THE
OIL
AND
VINEGAR
COMPANION

A CONNOISSEUR'S GUIDE

by
Kathryn Hawkins

THE
OIL
AND
VINEGAR
COMPANION

A CONNOISSEUR'S GUIDE

by
Kathryn Hawkins

RUNNING PRESS
PHILADELPHIA · LONDON

A QUINTET BOOK

9 8 7 6 5 4 3 2 1
Digit on the right indicates the number of this printing.

Library of Congress Control Number: 9780762434190
ISBN: 978-0-7624-3419-0

Publisher: James Tavendale
Managing Editor: Donna Gregory
Project Editor: Asha Savjani
Designer: Rod Teasdale
Photographer: Nick Wright
Art Director: Sofia Henry
Art Editor: Michael Charles
Editorial Assistant: Robert Davies
Proofreader: Angela Koo

Running Press Book Publishers
2300 Chestnut Street, Philadelphia, PA 19103-4371

Visit us on the web!
www.runningpresscooks.com

CONTENTS

INTRODUCTION

Mozzarella and tomato salad drizzled with olive oil

There are many successful marriages between different foods, and oil and vinegar is one of the most natural and harmonious. Like the best relationships, oils and vinegars have so much in common: they have both been around for thousands of years, they are versatile and have been used in the kitchen, in medicines, and beauty preparations for centuries, and there are many varieties of each. The appeal of oils and vinegars is still as strong today as it has been for thousands of years, and as they evolve to meet changing consumer tastes, oils and vinegars are amongst some of the most exciting and delicious culinary products of the last decade or so.

Edible oils have been used to enrich the diet for centuries. As methods of extraction and production have improved and advanced, we are now able to rediscover the benefits of many vegetable-based oils that were once enjoyed by our ancestors, several of which are proving to be excellent sources of micronutrients as well as adding different flavors and variety to our diet. Just about every delicatessen and grocery store has a wide range of oils on offer, ranging from old and familiar favorites like olive oil (see page 58) and sesame oil (see page 42) to lesser known oils like avocado oil (see page 54) and macadamia nut oil (see page 40). Some oils offer delicious flavor surprises like argan oil (see page 30) with its nutty aroma and rich seedy flavor, or plum kernel oil (see page 81) which smells and tastes like marzipan.

Vinegar is a very ancient ingredient. It more than likely evolved all on its own, by a quirk of nature. Once man began to brew his own wines and beers, it was only a matter of time before his prized liquor spoiled due to lack of know-how and poor storage—all fruit juices and lightly alcoholic liquids will turn sour once exposed to the air. He soon discovered that his spoiled wine had its own uses; thus vinegar was born and started life as a preservative. All over the world, vinegars are made from different cereals, plants, fruit, and vegetables, ranging from commonly available ingredients like rice and grains, to the more exotic coconut and sugar palm vinegars (see pages 124–5), and honey (see page 137) and maple syrup (see page 142) varieties.

Fresh green salad and oils

This companion sets out to guide you through the history of oils and vinegars and their development over the years. There is a brief commentary on how they are made and processed, how they are chemically structured, and how they can be used both in the kitchen and in other ways. There is a directory of the edible oils used today, some commonly available, whilst others are more obscure and are used in only remote, local communities. You will see, however, that as our knowledge continues to grow, there is potential for several of the lesser-known oils to become more widely produced and exported all round the globe. Each entry gives a description of the plant, how the oil is extracted, and how it can be used. There are also useful tasting and other descriptive notes, along with details of their nutritional composition.

Following on from the oil guide, you will find an equally useful description of different vinegars and similar acidic condiments. Each vinegar has a brief description of how it is made, followed by tasting notes, and descriptions of color, texture, and how it can be used. Following on from the guides, you'll find some classic recipes and a handy guide to pairing different oils and vinegars so you can experiment with flavor combinations. Finally, included in the back of the book, is a list of suppliers to help you track down oils and vinegars for your sampling.

There are more varieties of the condiments than I'd ever thought about before I embarked on my journey "around the world" of oils and vinegars; I've learnt a lot from my research and have certainly broadened my culinary repertoire accordingly. I hope you enjoy reading through the guide and learning more about the fascinating choice of oils and vinegars available to use today, and I hope that you will be tempted into trying some different varieties for yourself.

WARNING: If you have a nut or seed allergy check with your doctor before using any of the nut- or seed-based oils that are featured in this book.

An Introduction
to Oils

EDIBLE OILS—A BRIEF HISTORY

Palm oil plantation

In the warmer places of the world, vegetable, nut, and seed oils have been used for thousands of years. The ancient Egyptians show the seeds of the sesame plant, date palms, and olive branches in the hieroglyphics inside the tombs of the kings and queens of their time. It is also believed that they used oil from flax seeds as well as from the seeds of the benoil tree (also known as *moringa* nuts) and from castor beans. Nowadays, the latter two oils are used in industry only, although castor oil is also used medicinally and is most widely known as an infamous purgative. Coconut oil has been an important oil to South-east Asian regions of the world since records began, and similarly palm oil has been important to the African continent. Palm trees were successfully introduced to South-east Asia in the 19th century and plantations soon became a familiar sight; today, the oil has become a major commercial crop in this area.

In many parts of northern Europe and the US, oil is still a relatively new cooking ingredient. Small bottles of olive and almond oil were something you'd buy from the pharmacist for medicinal purposes until the 1970s. Hard fats like butter, lard, suet, and margarine, were much more commonly used in cooking and these fats form an essential part of the culinary history of the US. The use of non-vegetable fats developed because the climate was unsuitable for growing oilseed crops, and the pasture-rich land was much more suited to raising animals. In areas farther north still, where fishing was the main source of food production, the local diet consisted mainly of marine fats.

Over the last 100 years or so, there has been a decline in the consumption of animal fats in the diet, and a rise in vegetable oils. This is due to several causes. Oil grain and seed crops have been developed to suit other climates and production techniques have been improved. There has been a huge increase in the global export and import market for different foodstuffs. Worldwide travel has become something that most of us can afford and gives us the opportunity to experience other cuisines while on holiday. Exciting food writers like Elizabeth David, who appeared on the scene in the 1950s with her famous cookery book on Mediterranean food, have encouraged us to try out these different flavors in our own homes. Probably the most important reason of all is that there have been many nutritional discoveries about fats and oils and how they affect our bodies, and the consumer has demanded more choice for health reasons. Today, it is possible to find a huge range of edible oils in many stores and retail outlets.

Without doubt, the olive tree has made the biggest contribution to the history of edible oil, and it is probably the first oil one would think of when asked about popular oils for cooking (see page 58). The olive tree has its origins in Asia Minor—from the eastern Mediterranean coast across to modern day Iran. Cultivation records vary in time from between 5000 to

Olive tree

3500 B.C. Some reports say olive trees were first grown in Crete from where they spread to the Holy Land and the modern day Middle East. Other references suggest cultivation began in Mesopotamia (a vast fertile plain between the Tigris and Euphrates rivers, now known as Iraq) and spread via Turkey and Crete to Egypt, Greece, and farther westward across the Mediterranean. Alternatively, other records say olive tree cultivation could have begun even earlier, around 6000 B.C., in the region of modern day Palestine and Lebanon, much closer to the Mediterranean.

What is known for certain is that olives and their oil have played an important part in world history, with references made to them in the tombs of the ancient pharaohs and the Bible. The olive branch has been a symbol of glory, honor, and peace since the times of the ancient Greeks. An olive branch was awarded to the first Olympic athletes, along with the oil, and was a highly regarded prize. In 1500 B.C., Greece (particularly Mycenae) was the area where olive trees were most heavily cultivated. As the colonies expanded, interest in the olive tree reached southern Italy in the 8th century B.C. and then spread into southern France.

The "golden age" for olive growing came with the rise of the Roman Empire. The Romans planted olive trees in Spain and then across the entire Mediterranean basin. The Spanish, in turn, took the olive tree to the Americas in the 16th century. By the end of the century, Mexico was producing olive crops, and soon the trees were planted in Peru, Chile, and then in Argentina, where they were particularly well suited to the climate. In the 18th century, the olive tree was introduced to the US by Franciscan missionaries, and olive groves can still be seen up and down the Californian coastline today.

It would seem that olive oil and other pressed nut and seed oils have been around forever, yet the more mainstream oils we now know, and use every day, have a relatively recent past. In the 19th century, soybeans were first introduced to the US from China, where they

Soybeans

Rape crop field

had been growing for centuries. After the beans became established, they were first used as a coffee replacement and then as cattle feed. By the turn of the following century, nutritional studies were begun on the properties of this seemingly humble bean and it was soon recognized that the soybean had lots to offer nutritionally, both for its high protein and its low fat content. By the middle of the 20th century, soybean oil (see page 88) had become the most popular vegetable oil in the US. Today, soybean oil is the largest of all oil crops in the world.

Back in the early 20th century, Procter & Gamble researchers learned how to extract and refine the oil from cotton seeds (see page 57), a by-product of the linen industry. They developed a method to make the oil solid at room temperature as an alternative to natural lard, and the process of hydrogenation was born. Compared to the lard and other animal products of the day, this new product called *Crisco* was cheaper, easier to use, and could be stored at room temperature for 2 years without turning rancid.

Another well-known oil of the modern day is rapeseed oil (see page 44). Far from being a recent product, rapeseed oil has been used as a fuel by many people in Asia and Europe for thousands of years. Later, it was used in food as a cooking oil. Although grown as a crop in the 13th century, its potential wasn't fully recognized until the development of steam power, when it began to be used as a lubricant. During World War II, when blockades prevented the export of the oil across the Atlantic and Pacific oceans, Canada became a major producer, and has remained so ever since. Up until this time it was still unpopular as a food oil because it had a bitter taste caused by its erucic acid content. In the mid-1970s, Canadian researchers developed a low-erucic rapeseed cultivar for food use. Because the word "rape" was not considered optimal for marketing, a new name was coined—canola oil, the name being derived from "CANadian Oil, Low Acid" (see page 46). It soon became a popular culinary oil, and is now one of the most widely used oils in the world.

As you will soon see, there are many oils available to us today, with many uses. In the kitchen, some oils such as soybean, peanut (see page 34), and canola oil can be heated to high temperatures and are suitable for frying—both shallow- and deep-frying—and Oriental stir-frying. These oils can be added to marinades or brushed over less fatty food to help prevent drying during broiling, roasting, or barbecuing. These oils have little flavor of their own and so don't impart anything other than nutrients and calories to the food that is cooked with them. Other oils are used more specifically to enrich and add flavor to recipes like batters, cake mixes, sauces, and dressings, which are often infused with oil as an aromatic ingredient. Some oils also add color as well as their flavor and aroma. Finally, there are a few oils that can tolerate no heat at all, which are sprinkled over prepared food for their nutritional qualities, as well as imparting their own unique flavor.

Since ancient times, olive oil has been used by people to enhance strength and youth. It was infused with flowers and grasses to produce both medicines and cosmetics by the Egyptians, Greeks, and Romans. Today, outside the kitchen, olive oil is used in the cosmetic industry along with many other nut and seed oils. The nutritional makeup of these oils means they are quickly absorbed by the skin, adding nourishment and moisture. These oils make excellent carriers for more volatile oils and are used medicinally to treat a wide range of symptoms as part of a health and beauty aromatherapy treatment.

Cosmetic essential oils

OIL EXTRACTION AND PROCESSING

Cold pressing

The best gastronomic oils are those extracted simply, usually by a method called "cold pressing," where the oil is literally crushed out of the fruit or nut. This is the method used for virgin olive oil, seed, and nut oils. Centuries ago, this was done using the feet to stamp on the fruit until the oil exuded and could be collected. This system evolved into crushing by hand using a mortar and pestle, and then using millstones to grind the oil out of the fruit. The resulting oil is quickly filtered or left unfiltered, and then bottled as soon as possible, in dark glass or cans to protect it from the light. Cold-pressed oil retains some of the flavor of its origin; it is nutritious, richly colored, and highly aromatic. Cold-pressed oils are not processed in any other way, nor do they have anything added to them. They are expensive and highly valued for their delicious flavors. However, these oils do not keep well, and are not able to withstand heat; they are best used after cooking as a condiment, flavoring, or as an enriching agent.

Not all the oil can be removed during cold pressing, so the crushed mass is heated or has hot water added to it in order to make the remaining oil easier to remove. After this, solvents can be used to further "wash" the oil out. But, inevitably, the more something is processed, the fewer the characteristics of the original fruit that remain in the resulting oil, and the resulting oil often contains substances that give it a bad flavor—this then has to be removed by further processing. Other oil-producing foodstuffs, like those of oilseed origin (in particular cotton seed and rapeseed) initially have a less pleasing taste and color, and they also contain inedible impurities. They require oil extraction using heat or solvent chemicals. Soybean oil is extracted by centrifugal means, rather like salad leaves in a salad spinner. All oils extracted by heat, solvent, and centrifugal methods need to be refined in order to make them edible. This involves treatment by means of alkali neutralization in order to remove impurities, bleaching with fuller's earth to remove pigments, and finally deodorizing with steam. These various processes result in an all-round blander oil, which is often decolorized, and has very little of its original flavor or smell remaining.

One other method used is the expeller or screw-press system, which removes oil using mechanical pressure. It is used for extracting vegetable oils with a high oil content. During the pressing, the pressure creates heat that "melts" the plant tissue and releases the oil. The oil drips through holes in the press and can then be collected. Many years ago, these batch presses had to be filled up and emptied each time, but today, in modern plants, the presses operate continuously and have a much greater capacity for producing oils.

One farther processing technique that can be applied to oils after they have been refined is the industrial technique of hydrogenation. This involves "hardening" an oil so it becomes solid at room temperature, leaving its usual liquid state. The process heats the oil and uses hydrogen to alter its chemical structure. The hydrogen atoms attach themselves to carbon atoms at their weak double bonds, and thus turn them into strong single bonds. The resulting solid fat is more stable, less likely to

Extracting oil

turn rancid, and has a chemical and nutritional structure similar to saturated animal fats like butter and lard. For more information on the structure and nutrition of fats and oils, see page 18.

Preserved olive pulp

STORING AND USING OILS

Storing oils

One thing that most oils have in common is that once they are exposed to air they will turn rancid, develop an unpleasant smell and taste, and should be discarded. As we have already learnt, cold-pressed oils are the most vulnerable to oxidation, but even refined oils can deteriorate if not treated properly. Polyunsaturated oils are more susceptible to deterioration than monounsaturated; these oils will keep for about 6 months while monounsaturated oils can keep for a year or more. Bright light and excessive warmth will help speed up the decline of an oil as well, by bleaching the color and destroying flavor and nutrients. It makes perfect sense, therefore, to store oils in a cool, dark place and to avoid open storage on kitchen worktops or in cupboards above the stove.

Purchase oils in small quantities in order to use them as quickly as possible. Alternatively, decant from a large bottle into smaller ones, in order to keep the bottles as full as possible. Ensure that the bottles are well sealed. Dark glass bottles, earthenware, or cans will offer the maximum protection for your chosen oil. Some fresh oils require refrigeration and have a short life of up to 6 weeks once opened—always read the label for the suggested storage instructions

SMOKE POINTS OF REFINED OILS SUITABLE FOR HIGH TEMPERATURE COOKING

Soybean oil	approx. 492°F	Groundnut oil	approx. 450°F
Canola oil	approx. 470°F	Sunflower	approx. 430°F
Canola oil (semi-refined)	approx. 465°F	Cotton seed oil	approx. 425°F
Corn oil	approx. 450°F	Palm oil	approx. 415°F
Safflower oil	approx. 445°F	Grapeseed oil	approx. 400°F

NOTE: Avocado oil has a very high smoke point of approximately 520°F, but its price and flavor make it an unlikely choice for deep-frying.

for each particular oil. Some oils like macadamia nut oil (see page 40) and extra virgin olive oil (see page 61) will turn cloudy and thick if they get too cold. Either stand at room temperature or immerse the bottle in slightly warm water (not hot) to return the oil to its clear, liquid state. This does not affect the oil in any way and it will be perfectly safe to consume afterward.

Most fats and oils begin to deteriorate well below their individual boiling points, and their ability to withstand heating determines their usefulness in different cooking methods. Oils suitable for deep-frying are able to sustain more intense heating before the fat begins to break down into visible gases—this point of change is referred to as the "smoke point." Oils should not be heated beyond their individual smoke point (see table on facing page), because the longer an oil is heated for, the quicker it begins to decompose. It is best, therefore, to avoid preheating an oil for longer than is necessary. Choose the tallest, deepest pan suitable for deep-frying in order to reduce the surface area of the oil that is exposed to the air. If you are cooking in batches, try to cook each batch in the hot oil as soon after the previous batch has finished cooking as possible, then take the oil off the heat immediately to cool. Oil can be re-used once or twice if it has not passed its smoke point and has been filtered clean—either through cheesecloth or a paper coffee filter. Remember that reheated oil will have a lower smoke point than when in its original state, so it should be reheated and re-used accordingly. For re-use, allow the oil to cool completely in the pan, filter it, and pour it through a funnel into a clean bottle. Always cool the oil completely, as hot oil will melt through a plastic container very quickly. Always discard oil that has reached its smoke point or has become cloudy, smelly, or tainted. Do not pour oil down the drain. Instead, decant it back into its original bottle or other suitable container, seal well, and put it in the garbage or a designated recycling collection point.

Deep-frying shrimp

BASIC OIL CHEMISTRY AND NUTRITION

Oil—a liquid fat

In order to understand oils properly, it helps to know something of their chemical makeup. It is important to understand the differences between oils so that you can make an informed choice to suit your personal nutritional needs.

Structure of fats and oils

Fats and oils are members of the lipid family. The only difference between a fat and an oil is that a fat is solid at room temperature, whereas an oil is liquid. An oil, therefore, is simply a liquid fat. In cooking terms, fats and oils make food more palatable, giving it texture, richness, and flavor; fat makes you feel satisfied after eating it. For the body, fat provides calories, and lots of them. In truth, the body doesn't need much fat at all, just a few grams a day to provide it with the fat-soluble vitamins A, D, E, and K and other unique fat-bound substances called essential fatty acids. When you eat more fat than your body needs, it gets stored and leads to weight gain and eventually obesity, along with other related diseases (the risk of developing these is heightened by the type of fat ingested).

Fatty acids and triglycerides

A fatty acid molecule is made up of carbon, hydrogen, and oxygen atoms, usually arranged in a chain. Each atom of carbon in the chain can be linked to 2 hydrogen atoms—the atoms at the end of the chain do not link—and where this occurs, the chain will be strong and less subject to change. If 2 carbon atoms side-by-side do not link with hydrogen atoms they will join on to each other and form a "double bond;" this makes a weak point in the chain and means that the fat is less stable and more susceptible to change. There are many fatty acids, and all fats and oils are made up of specific combinations; some fatty acids form short chains of 4 carbons whilst others may be long and heavy, and up to 35 carbons long. Short- and medium-chained fats are liquid at room temperature, whilst longer chains make the fat solid.

Lipids (fats and oils) form chemical compounds called triglycerides. Triglycerides are so called because they are made up of 3 fatty acid molecules and a single molecule of an alcohol (glycerol) more commonly known as glycerine. Glycerine is a short, 3-carbon chain onto which the fatty acids attach themselves. The particular properties of a fat or oil depend on the triglycerides it contains.

Saturated, unsaturated, monounsaturated, and polyunsaturated

We see the above terms on just about all the fats we buy these days, and it can be very confusing knowing what each definition means and how it can affect your health. Here is a simple explanation:

- A saturated fatty acid is made up of a carbon chain with a full complement of hydrogen atoms. The chain has no double bonds. This type of fatty acid is very straight and regularly formed, and can form some of the longest carbon chains. The solid chain gives a solid structure, meaning that the fat will be solid at room temperature. No natural fat is completely saturated—if it were, it would be very hard and brittle; a solid animal fat, like butter, contains about 60 percent saturated fatty acids.

- An unsaturated fatty acid has one or more double bonds between its carbon atoms in the chain. If it has one double bond only, it is known as *monounsaturated*, and if it has 2 or more it is called *polyunsaturated*. The more double bonds there are in the chain, the more kinks or weaknesses that form—this gives a less stable compound and affects the stability of the fat itself. For instance, it is relatively easy for the chains to be disrupted by oxygen and cause the fat to become rancid. Vegetable-based oils are usually mono- and polyunsaturated, although, conversely, coconut and palm oils are very saturated, while fish oils are unsaturated.

Rapeseed oil

Hydrogenation and trans-fatty acids

This is a process invented on a commercial scale to help stabilize certain fats. Unsaturated fats or oils are less stable because they have less hydrogen in their fatty acids. Hydrogenation is carried out by heating the fat under extreme pressure using nickel as a catalyst. During this process hydrogen is added and some of the kinks and weaknesses are straightened out by untwisting the double bonds to make them less extreme. The new positioning of the atoms in the chain is called "trans," and so they become known as trans-fatty acids. Fats hydrogenated in this way are transformed from liquid unsaturated oil into a saturated hard fat with a longer shelf life and a higher melting point, but they also take on less desirable nutritional properties (see page 22). Because of the medical implications of eating too much saturated fat, manufacturers are developing new processing techniques to replace the old hydrogenation process, so that soft fats and oil can be hardened without the production of trans-fatty acids.

Essential fatty acids: Omega 3, 6, and 9

Essential fatty acids (EFAs) are a vital part of our daily nutrition, and just like certain vitamins and minerals, our intake of EFAs must come from a balanced diet in order to maintain good health. Our bodies cannot make EFAs, so we must ingest them in our food. These essential fatty acids are involved in specific biological roles in the body and are different from the more common fatty acids which, more simply, provide us with fuel (calories) and act as carriers for vitamins. EFAs are long-chain polyunsaturated fatty acids derived from linolenic, linoleic, and oleic acids. They are divided into different families: omega-3, omega-6, and omega-9, although the latter is necessary yet "non-essential" because the body can manufacture a modest amount on its own, provided the other essential EFAs are present. Their number derives from the position of the first double bond from the end of the chain e.g. an omega-3 unsaturated fatty acid has its first double bond beginning at the third carbon atom from the end of the chain. Omega-3 fatty acids are derived from linolenic acid, omega-6 from linoleic acid, and omega-9 from oleic acid.

Omega-3 (Linolenic Acid)—Alpha Linolenic Acid (ALA) is the principal omega-3 fatty acid. Omega-3s are used in the formation of cell walls, making them supple and flexible, and ensuring and improving the circulation and oxygen uptake of red blood cells in the body. Omega-3 deficiencies are linked to several conditions such as poor memory, tingling sensation of the nerves, poor vision, increased tendency to form blood clots, impaired immune system, increased triglycerides and "bad" cholesterol (LDL) levels, hypertension, irregular heartbeat, and growth retardation. The best ALA source is flax seed oil (see page 41) and 1/2 fl oz of this oil a day will provide the body with the minimum 1/4 oz ALA it requires for health.

Argan oil and nuts

Omega-6 (Linoleic Acid)—Linoleic Acid is the primary omega-6 fatty acid. Some omega-6 improves diabetic neuropathy, rheumatoid arthritis, PMS, skin disorders, and aids healing in cancer treatment. Although we may consume ample omega-6 fatty acids, the modern day diet and environment we live in have detrimental effects on our uptake of this particular EFA. Diets rich in sugar, alcohol, or trans fats from processed foods, as well as smoking, pollution, stress, ageing, viral infections, and other illnesses such as diabetes, often impair our body's ability to use these EFAs properly. Flax seed oil is rich in linoleic acid and other sources include hemp (see page 51), grapeseed (see page 33), and olive oil (see page 58). Unrefined oils from corn (see page 93), safflower (see page 80), sunflower (see page 74), and soybean (see page 88) are also good sources, but the refining process can eliminate a lot of their nutritional value.

Omega-9 (Oleic Acid)—Technically not an EFA, because the human body can manufacture a limited amount of omega-9 provided other essential EFAs are present, but it is important and worth mentioning here. Monounsaturated oleic acid lowers the risk of heart attack and arteriosclerosis, and helps with cancer prevention. Oleic acid is found primarily in olive oil and extra virgin olive oil and also in sesame oil (see page 42).

CAUTION

High heat, direct light, and oxygen destroy EFAs, so when using oils for their EFA content, avoid cooking with them or using them on excessively hot food. Store these oils in well-sealed containers in a cool place and out of the light, and choose oils in dark glass, earthenware, or metal containers for extra protection. See individual entries for specific storage recommendations.

Omega-3 fatty acids from certain oils play an important role in controlling LDL levels in the blood

Cholesterol

This is a waxy substance of the lipid family that is made by our bodies in the liver. Cholesterol particles link with carrier proteins in the bloodstream (lipoproteins) which then take them all round the body. When the blood has too much cholesterol in it, health problems can occur. Deposits of cholesterol can build up in the arteries of various parts of the body, but particularly around the heart, and can cause the blood flow to be restricted; this is the disease called atherosclerosis. When this disease is present, the blood is unable to provide the nutrients and oxygen the heart (or other organs) needs to function properly so the muscle supporting the heart begins to fail. In severe cases, there is a danger that a rupture may occur, leading to blood clots breaking away and causing a blockage. This may lead to a heart attack, stroke, or even sudden death.

However, the cholesterol in our bodies can be controlled by what we eat. Lipoproteins can be divided into 2 categories: low-density (LDL) and high-density (HDL). These different types work in completely opposite ways to each other. LDL or "bad cholesterol" takes cholesterol away from the liver in the blood and deposits it in different places, whereas the HDL or "good cholesterol" takes the cholesterol back to the liver where it can be processed and then eliminated from the body. The more HDL you have in your bloodstream, the less chance there is that you will develop deposits of cholesterol in your arteries. Omega-3 fatty acids have an important function in controlling LDL levels in the blood.

Directory
of Oils

BRAZIL NUT OIL

The Amazon nut or castana is known commercially as the Brazil nut. It is the seed of one the great canopy trees of the Amazonian rain forest. The Brazil nut tree, *Bertholletia excelsa*, which stands up to 150 feet tall, is found mainly in the Amazon basin of South America where it grows in deep, well-drained soil on high ground. Rare euglossine bees pollinate the flowers of the tree. After flowering is complete, the nuts form in large pods weighing 3 to 4 pounds each and containing between 12 and 20 kernels per pod. Trees start producing nuts when they reach 12 to 15 years old. The fruit containing the angular kernels takes a year to ripen. The ripe kernels contain about 65 percent oil. Countries such as Brazil, Venezuela, Guyana, Bolivia, Colombia, and Peru are all major producers of Brazil nuts.

AT-A-GLANCE INFO

NUTRITIONAL HIGHLIGHT: Rich in oleic acid (Om-9) and linoleic acid (Om-6)

COUNTRY OF ORIGIN: Amazon basin region of South America

STORAGE: As with all nut and seed oils, store out of direct light. The shelf life is usually about 12 to 18 months, but check the use by label.

ALTERNATIVE: Hazelnut oil

RECOMMENDED: Living Organic Cold-Pressed Extra Virgin Brazil nut oil—Amazon Flame® or Candela Organic Brazil Nut Oil from Peru

The Brazil nut tree is a good example of the intricate ecosystem of the Amazon, where plants and animals live and work alongside each other. Not only is the pollination of this tree very specialized, requiring one particular insect species to produce the fruit, but only one species of animal, a large rodent called an agouti, is capable of chewing through the extremely tough fruit pod to disperse the seeds for new tree growth. In the rain forest, the tree, bee, and agouti are all dependent on one another for survival. Virtually all Brazil nut production comes from wild forest trees and wild harvesting. The trees grow very slowly and, coupled with their specific pollination, this makes them unsuitable and unprofitable for plantation cultivation.

In Brazil, mature nuts fall between November and early June. Harvesting is done by manual labor. Each summer, approximately 1,000 families come to the rain forest to harvest these Amazon nuts. Mature pods fall to the ground and are collected in baskets. Harvesting also depends on the weather, as pods will only be gathered if there is little or no wind, to minimize the danger of people being hit by falling pods. The pods are washed and sometimes dried before storage. Drying is usually carried out in a primitive shelter although this is often difficult as nuts are collected during the rainy season. Pods are often simply stored piled in heaps. On a large production site, however, pods are dried using large forced-air driers.

For centuries, Brazil nuts have been used locally in traditional medicine and folklore. Today, they are a highly valued commodity, and are mainly collected for export. Brazil nuts are used in the snack industry, in confectionery, and in baking. The pods are cut open with a long sharp knife called a *tercado*. The nuts are then soaked for 24 hours before a short boiling, which allows the nut shells to be removed by hand. The shelled nuts are then stored in cool, dark conditions to prevent them turning rancid. Only surplus or damaged nuts are used for processing into Brazil nut oil.

In the past, Brazil nut oil has been utilized mainly by the cosmetic industry. The extraction of this oil is currently carried out because of its highly nutritional benefits. Heat alters the oil's fine structure, and impairs the taste and some of its nutritional content. Due to a low-temperature extraction process, most Brazil nut oil has never been heated or refined. It is a clear, yellowish oil with a pleasant, sweet smell and nutty taste.

Brazil nut oil contains mainly palmitic, oleic, and linoleum acids and small amounts of myristic and stearic acids and phytosterols. In addition to protein and fat, Brazil nuts provide the highest natural source of selenium—an essential trace mineral in the human body with antioxidant and cancer-preventing properties. One single Brazil nut exceeds the US Recommended Daily Allowance of selenium for adults. The proteins found in Brazil nuts are very high in sulfur-containing amino acids like methionine. The presence of this type of amino acid enhances the absorption of selenium and other minerals in the nut.

In the kitchen, Brazil nut oil is best added to a finished dish in order to preserve the oil's nutritional status. It makes a wonderful light oil for salad dressings—try combining it with raspberry vinegar for a tasty vinaigrette to dress an exotic fruit salad. In addition, Brazil nut oil is often used in soaps, shampoos, and hair conditioning/repairing products as well as in skin moisturizers.

WALNUT OIL

Walnut oil is regarded as one of the finest nuts grown in temperate regions. There are many varieties, but the most important is *Juglans regia*, the English walnut (or Persian walnut). It is a large, elegant tree that grows in south-east Europe and throughout temperate Asia. Walnut oil was one of the most important oils to Renaissance painters because it dries quickly and doesn't leave a yellow tint. Nowadays, flax seed oil (see page 41) and poppy oil (see page 48) are preferred because they have better storage qualities. Wild walnuts have been harvested for thousands of years and eaten as food. They were highly prized by the Romans who served them at various ceremonial feasts and occasions.

The fruit of the walnut tree is a green drupe with flesh surrounding a hard-shelled nut. Inside this is the oil-rich kernel. The fruit can be picked at various stages of its development depending on what it is being used for. Sour green walnuts are used for pickling and other preserves; half-ripe walnuts can be shelled and

AT-A-GLANCE INFO

NUTRITIONAL HIGHLIGHT: Rich in linoleic acid (Om-6)

COUNTRY OF ORIGIN: Primarily France

STORAGE: As with all nut and seed oils, store out of direct light. The shelf life is usually about 12 to 18 months.

ALTERNATIVE: Hazelnut oil

RECOMMENDED: Try Clearspring Organic Walnut Oil—or Cuisine de Provence Walnut Oil.

Organic green salad with walnut and lime-pepper dressing

are preserved in syrup in the Middle East; and fully ripe walnuts are usually available whole, in their shells, or with the shell removed and packed as half kernels or walnut kernel pieces.

For oil production, ripe walnuts are stored for several weeks to dry them out—this is unusual amongst other nut and seed oils which require immediate processing. During this time, the milky juice turns into a light, clean oil with an oily, nutty aroma and distinctive walnut flavor. Most walnut oil is produced in France, particularly in the Perigord and Burgundy regions, though there are also producers in Australia, New Zealand, and California.

Walnut oil is not used as extensively as other oils in the kitchen. It is expensive and has a rich, nutty taste. It is best used unheated as a flavoring rather than a cooking oil. When it is heated, it can become slightly bitter and

it will lose heat-sensitive antioxidants. Some woodworkers favor walnut oil as a finish for implements that will come into contact with food, such as chopping boards and wooden bowls. It is also used as a moisturizer for mature skin and dry scalps.

HAZELNUT OIL

The common wild hazel, *Corylus avellana*, is a species of hazel native to Europe and south-west Asia. It is a low, shrub-like tree, which often forms part of a hedgerow. The scientific name *avellana* derives from the town of Avellino in Italy where the hazelnut tree was first cultivated during the early 17th century. Today the common hazel is cultivated for its nuts in commercial orchards across Europe, as well as in Turkey, Iran, and the Caucasus. The top producer is Turkey, accounting for approximately 75 percent of worldwide production. In the US, hazelnut production is concentrated in 2 states: Oregon and Washington; however, hazelnuts are also grown extensively just to the north, in the Fraser Valley of British Columbia, Canada. California is also another possible production region for the future. Hazelnuts are grown extensively in Australia in orchards growing varieties that are mostly imported from Europe.

The name "hazelnut" is applied to the nuts of any of the species of the genus *Corylus*. The kernel of the seed is edible and used raw or roasted, or ground into a paste. The seed has a

AT-A-GLANCE INFO

NUTRITIONAL HIGHLIGHT: Rich in oleic acid (Om-9)

COUNTRY OF ORIGIN: Europe and south-west Asia

STORAGE: Store away from direct sunlight, and always make sure the bottle is well sealed after use. Hazelnut oil has a shelf life of about 12 months, but always check the use by date.

ALTERNATIVE: 1 part walnut oil mixed with 2 parts sunflower oil

RECOMMENDED: Try La Tourangelle Roasted Hazelnut oil or Cuisine de Provence Hazelnut Oil brands.

Hazelnut butter

thin, dark brown skin, which has a bitter flavor and is sometimes removed before cooking.

Hazelnuts are harvested annually in mid fall when the trees drop their nuts and leaves. Most commercial growers wait for the nuts to drop on their own, rather than using equipment to shake them from the tree. The harvesting is either by hand in rural communities, or by the manual or mechanical raking of fallen nuts on a commercial scale. Hazelnuts are usually used as a nut in their own right for bakery and baking products, in confectionery to make praline, and in combination with chocolate to make truffles and spreads. In the US, hazelnut butter is being promoted as a more nutritious spread than peanut butter. The oil pressed from hazelnuts is regarded as one of the greatest culinary oils.

The process of extracting the oil is a traditional one which has not changed for centuries. The hazelnuts are ground and roasted in cast-iron kettles to make a warm paste. This is then pressed in a hydraulic press. Following mechanical extraction, the oil is lightly filtered and bottled. The leftover press cake is used as animal feed.

Hazelnut oil is lightly golden with a fresh, mildly nutty aroma; it tastes buttery and creamy rich, with a hint of the nut itself. Suitable for use over medium-high heat, you can use it for sautéing and baking, or drizzling on a finished dish. It is delicious in salads and combines very well with vinegar to produce a light but flavorful vinaigrette. It is the perfect match for verjuice (see page 115). With pasta, potatoes, and beans, it makes an excellent substitute for butter. Try it with fish or cheese, or as a dipping oil for fresh bread. If you have a sweet tooth, it makes wonderful cakes and cookies—and try adding it to ice cream for added creaminess.

Nutritionally, the fatty acid composition of hazelnut oil corresponds exactly to that of olive oil, providing the same high oleic acid content.

ARGAN OIL

Argan oil is produced from the seeds of the fruit of the argan tree, *Argania sideroxylon* and *Argania spinosa,* which is native to North Africa. Today, the trees grow wild in arid semi-desert conditions in south-west Morocco where they are known as the "tree of life" because they can support the local population and its livestock during times of drought. The fruit sustains goats, the leaves provide forage for camels and sheep, whilst cattle live off the press cake that remains after the oil has been made.

Argan trees can have a single trunk, or a number of twisted, thickened stems and can grow up to a height of 30 feet. They yield the most fruit after 50 to 60 years, often surviving for 200 to 250 years and making the trees a valuable inheritance for future generations. The trees flower in the spring, producing green, olive-sized fruits that ripen to yellow. Harvesting takes place in September and there

AT-A-GLANCE INFO

NUTRITIONAL HIGHLIGHT: Good source of linoleic acid (Om-6) and vitamin E. Contains unique plant sterols, believed to have anti-inflammatory properties, beneficial for arthritic and rheumatic conditions.

COUNTRY OF ORIGIN: Morocco

STORAGE: Choose argan oil which is sold in dark glass or frosted bottles to protect it from light and store it away from direct sunlight. Use by the date on the label, but it usually has a shelf life of about 18 months.

ALTERNATIVE: 1 part sesame oil to 3 parts sunflower oil

RECOMMENDED: Belazu Organic Argan Oil

Warm salad: avocado, eggs, Roquefort, bacon, and argan oil

are 2 methods used to harvest argan fruit in addition to shaking the tree and collecting the fruits from the ground. Grazing goats sometimes eat the fallen fruits, spitting out the seeds, which are then gathered up by hand. Camels are also fed the fruits—the seeds are indigestible and pass through the animal to be excreted and gathered from the dung. The trees have sharp spiny thorns, which prevent the fruit from being picked by hand. Owners of livestock are forbidden to let their animals graze in the argan groves for 3 months before and during the harvest—in the past, goats climbed the thorny branches to eat the fruit, so much so that the groves were known locally as tree meadows. The groves are now protected.

Argan oil has been used for centuries in Morocco because of its health-giving properties. The oil is clear and richly brown in color with a nutty aroma. The flavor is more like toasted seeds, reminiscent of sesame, but not as pungent. It is best to add argan oil to dishes after cooking in order to preserve the nutrients. Drizzle over broiled fish, chicken, and roasted vegetables, or as a finishing touch to barbecued food. It makes an excellent salad dressing, with or without lemon juice or vinegar. Add extra nuttiness to vegetable dips and hummus by adding a little to the finished mix. Try it in soups as a rich finishing touch, drizzle over goat's cheese, or combine it with honey on top of thick plain yogurt, porridge, or muesli. In Morocco argan oil is usually eaten by Berber families with breakfast or as a teatime treat with homemade bread. It is made into an indulgent spread with almonds and honey, called *amalou*, and added to a porridge-like mixture called *sematar*, which is made from wheat germ and honey and eaten for breakfast.

ALMOND OIL

The almond tree has been cultivated since prehistoric times and the almond nut is one of the most important in the world of commerce. The US is the world's greatest producer, followed by Spain and Italy. Almonds are also grown across the Mediterranean, and in Greece, Iran, Australia, and Afghanistan.

Bitter and sweet almond varieties are grown. Sweet almonds, *Prunus amygdalus dulcis*, do not contain amygdalin (a glycocide) and are widely used as nuts and food ingredients. Bitter almonds do contain amygdalin and an enzyme that causes it to hydrolyze into glucose, benzaldehyde (the familiar almond aroma), and hydrocyanic acid (a very poisonous substance from which cyanide is obtained).

Almond oil is a delicate and expensive product, and is highly regarded as a superfine culinary oil. It is available from the pharmacy and some specialist suppliers. It is a good source of fatty acids and vitamins A, B1, B2, B6, and E. Commercially, it is widely used in the confectionery business as it has an exceptionally mild flavor and is clear and virtually colorless, making it ideal for greasing confectionery molds and surfaces where sticky sugar mixtures are prepared. Toasted almond oil has a nuttier flavor and makes a good choice for delicate fish dishes, herb salads, and sweet fruit. It is pale yellow in color and has a light "toasty" aroma.

AT-A-GLANCE INFO

NUTRITIONAL HIGHLIGHT: Linoleic acid (Om-6)

COUNTRY OF ORIGIN: North America, Europe

STORAGE: As with all nut and seed oils, store out of direct light. The shelf life is usually about 12 to 18 months.

ALTERNATIVE: Plum seed oil

RECOMMENDED: Cuisine de Provence Almond Oil or La Tourangelle Almond Oil

GRAPESEED OIL

The grape vine, *Vitis viniferous*, with its fleshy small bunches of fruit, is chiefly grown as a table fruit, dried fruit, or for the wine/juice industry in France, Spain, Italy, Chile, the US, and Australia.

Grape seeds are available as by-products of the aforementioned industries. In general each fruit contains 4 or 5 seeds. The oil content varies considerably between 6 and 21 percent, with sweet wine grape seeds yielding the most oil while some black varieties are at the lower end of the range. Because the quantity of grapes produced is so large, there is considerable potential for grapeseed oil extraction.

In recent years grapeseed oil has become nutritionally noted and is recommended for inclusion in diets designed for lowering cholesterol. Low in saturated fats and rich in vitamins and minerals, it has a very high linoleic acid content.

The light, bright, green oil is best used as a dressing oil or for shallow- and stir-frying. It would certainly add a dash of fresh color in a dressing and works well with any vinegar, as it will not overwhelm other ingredients.

As a cosmetic, grapeseed oil is suitable for all skin types and has good moisturizing and nourishing properties.

AT-A-GLANCE INFO

NUTRITIONAL HIGHLIGHT: Linoleic acid (Om-6)

COUNTRY OF ORIGIN: Europe, America, Australia

STORAGE: Store in a cool dry place away from direct sunlight for up to 12 months.

ALTERNATIVE: Sunflower oil for cooking; light olive oil for flavor and color

RECOMMENDED: Roland Grapeseed Oil and La Tourangelle Grapeseed Oil

PEANUT OIL

This oil often causes confusion in that peanut and groundnut oil are believed to be two different products. As a general everyday cooking oil, they are one and the same thing. However, in Chinese cooking, sometimes a different type of peanut oil is used as a dressing or finishing oil, and this is a different product altogether.

The common or garden Western peanut oil (for want of a better expression) comes from a leguminous species of plant. It was first grown in pre-Inca times in Peru and will thrive in tropical and sub-tropical conditions. It is now one of the world's major food crops for nutrition and commerce. India and China are the largest producers, but it is also a huge crop for the US. Peanuts are important in their own right and are sold whole as a snack food or for use in confectionery and the making of peanut butter, but they are also important for their oil.

Arachis hypogaea is the most common species of peanut and consists of several varieties. Once the plants have flowered and pollinated, the stems continue to develop underground where the fruit (nuts) form, all growing near the main roots. Each fruit consists of a pod-like pale brown shell, which dries on maturity and contains 2 to 4 kernels which we know as peanuts (also known as monkey nuts and earth nuts). Each kernel is encased in a thin red skin. The kernels contain 40 to 50 percent oil.

Peanut oil was used as the original source of fuel for the diesel engine. It is better known, however, as a much-used cooking oil. It has a silky texture and a very high smoke point—it is often used as a commercial deep-frying oil. It is pale gold in color and has little flavor, but a slight nutty flavor is detectable. It congeals at 41°F or below, but this doesn't affect its flavor or cooking properties. It is a good all rounder for shallow-frying, stir-frying, and deep-frying, and using as a light dressing oil. It is the perfect choice for blending with stronger flavored nut oils to make them go farther, enable them to be used in cooking, and to temper their strength of flavor; try a ratio of 1 part peanut to 4 parts sesame or walnut. Peanut oil also makes a tasty, light, slightly nutty mayonnaise. Cold-pressed peanut oil has a much fresher peanut aroma and flavor and can also be used for all methods of cooking, but will give a distinct "peanutty" flavor to your cooking. It has a shorter shelf life and should be stored at room temperature, out of the light.

Nutritionally speaking, peanut oil is made up of about 47 percent monounsaturated, 32 percent polyunsaturated, and about 20 percent saturated fatty acids. Its major component fatty acids are palmitic acid, oleic acid, and linoleic acid, but it also contains other fatty acids such as arachidic acid, arachidonic acid, behenic acid, and lignoceric acid.

There are 2 types of peanut oil - the lighter, paler colored cooking oil which is used widely and known in the UK as groundnut oil, and the oil you are likely to find in small bottles in an oriental supermarket. This second kind of peanut oil has a much stronger flavor of the nut than the general cooking oil of the same name. Sometimes the peanuts are roasted so the flavor is even more intense. The color is a richer golden to light brown. It is a much more expensive oil than general peanut oil and is used, like sesame oil (see page 42), not to cook with, but to season. This type of peanut oil has more in common with other nut oils like walnut (see page 26), and should be used with more restraint. In fact, it is worth thinking of it as a nut essence rather than an oil. It is perfect sprinkled over stir-fries, rice, and noodle dishes, or drizzled over a salad to give a nutty twist. It is also good with fruits like banana, mango, and papaya. It has the same nutritional composition as peanut oil.

Warning: Because groundnut oil is made from peanuts, people who suffer from any nut allergy should avoid it (and warn anyone cooking for them as well). However, commercial peanut oil is unlikely to cause an allergic reaction because the allergen is a protein, not a fat. The cold-pressed and organic oils will contain other extracts of the peanut, which are likely to cause a reaction. They are usually less filtered, retaining some peanut proteins for the sake of flavor and nutrition. Always seek medical advice if you have a peanut allergy before consuming this oil.

AT-A-GLANCE INFO

NUTRITIONAL HIGHLIGHT: Good source of oleic (Om-9) and linoleic acid (Om-6)

COUNTRY OF ORIGIN: Various

STORAGE: Store in a cool dry place. It keeps for about 12 months unopened, but once opened check the manufacturer's instructions.

ALTERNATIVE: 1 part sesame oil mixed with 2 parts groundnut oil

RECOMMENDED: Peanut oil is available widely and the Oriental variety is available from specialist stockists of Oriental products.

PECAN OIL

This is the most important nut of North America, originating from a type of hickory tree, which is related to the walnut. The pecan tree, *Caryocar nuciferum*, is native to central southern regions of the US, but it is now also cultivated in Israel, Mexico, South Africa, and Australia. It grows some 164 feet high and can live for up to 300 years. The fruit is a drupe, consisting of a very hard, smooth woody shell surrounding a fairy oily edible nut, which is similar to a walnut kernel but is milder and sweeter in flavor. The oil is pressed from the kernel.

Pecan oil is quite thick. It is silky smooth in texture and has a sweet, nutty flavor, less powerful than a walnut oil (see page 26). It is pale golden and clear in color. It blends well with white and traditional balsamic vinegar (see page 108), Vincotto® (see page 113), raspberry and other fruit vinegars (see page 145). Whilst it will increase the flavor of any dish containing nuts, it is delicious drizzled over a fruity dessert, yogurt, or soft cheese. Pecan oil is also recommended served with rice and polenta dishes, and is very tasty smeared over freshly cooked corn on the cob.

AT-A-GLANCE INFO

NUTRITIONAL HIGHLIGHT: Good source of linoleic acid (Om-6)

COUNTRY OF ORIGIN: Noth America, France

STORAGE: Store away from direct light for 6 to 12 months.

ALTERNATIVE: Hazelnut oil

RECOMMENDED: Try the French produced J. Leblanc Pecan Oil for a sweetly aromatic nut oil

PISTACHIO OIL

The small deciduous tree, *Pistacia vera*, native to parts of west Asia and the area between Turkey and Afghanistan, bears a highly sought-after fruit, dating back thousands of years. Pistachios are now cultivated in the eastern Mediterranean and also the US.

The tree can reach a height of 32 feet and live several hundred years. Generally it produces a good crop in alternate years. The fruit is a small, dry drupe, which looks a bit like an olive and grows in clusters. It has a hard, smooth outer shell, which splits open when ripe to reveal an edible yellowish or green nut, depending on variety. Color is an important indicator of quality: the greener the pistachio, the more highly prized and flavorful it is. Pistachios are unique amongst nuts in that the color is the same throughout due to the presence of chlorophyll.

One of the most expensive nut oils, it has a much stronger flavor than other oils. Like other nut oils, it tastes similar to the nut from which it is extracted—it is sweet with a distinct savory note. It is light amber in color and smells of roasted pistachios. Due to its pronounced flavor, this oil will easily overpower and doesn't go with everything. But, it can be used with sweet and savory dishes. Heat will alter the flavor, so it is best kept as a dressing or condiment oil.

AT-A-GLANCE INFO

NUTRITIONAL HIGHLIGHT: Good source of oleic acid (Om-9), linoleic acid (Om-6) and vitamin E

COUNTRY OF ORIGIN: Various

STORAGE: Store at room temperature out of direct light. Has a shelf life of about 2 years.

ALTERNATIVE: Argan oil or hazelnut oil

RECOMMENDED: Roland Roasted Pistachio Oil and A l'Olivier Pistachio Oil

PINE NUT OIL

There are many species of this familiar tree, but it is the *Pinus pinea* that grows wild across the Mediterranean and into the Middle East, from which the kernels are most commonly obtained for oil making. This familiar forest tree, parasol-shaped, can reach up to 98 feet in height. It has dark green clusters of needles. The fruit takes the form of a reddish brown cone. After about 3 years, as the scales of the cone open, they release winged, hard-shelled edible seeds or "nuts."

The oil pressed from these nuts is of a light, bright yellow color and sweet flavor. It tastes slightly nutty and mildly of pine and can be quite expensive. Pine nut oil has a relatively low smoke point, and is therefore not generally used during cooking. Rather, it is added to foods for "finishing," to add flavor. Try with avocados, broiled fish, goat's cheese, and shellfish. Add to pesto for an extra pine-nut kick. Pine nut oil was traditionally used in Russia during the period of Lent when the use of animal fats is forbidden. It is also used in the cuisine of southern France.

Pine nut oil is very rich in polyunsaturated fatty acids—it is about 50 percent linoleic acid. It is the richest and only known source of pinolenic acid, which is not present in any other species of plant, and is believed to help suppress the appetite and promote the feeling of "fullness."

AT-A-GLANCE INFO

NUTRITIONAL HIGHLIGHT: Good source of linoleic acid (Om-6); only known source of pinolenic acid

COUNTRY OF ORIGIN: various

STORAGE: Has a shelf life of about 1 year.

ALTERNATIVE: Hazelnut oil

RECOMMENDED: J. Leblanc Pine Nut Oil, Extra Virgin Siberian Pine Nut Oil

MACADAMIA NUT OIL

The *Macadamia integrifolia* and *M. tetraphylla* trees are indigenous to Australia, but they have now been introduced to other countries such as Hawaii, the US, parts of Africa, Guatemala, Costa Rica, Brazil, and Fiji.

Macadamia nuts have an oil content of about 60 percent. The oil is extracted using small expellers. This produces an edible oil which is also used in the cosmetic industry and to make soap. The press cake is used as animal feed. Macadamia oil is stable and has a high oleic acid and natural antioxidant (vitamin E) content. It is the richest plant source of palmitoleic acid, which is good for the skin. It is pale yellow in color and has a taste and smell similar to unprocessed macadamia nuts and a mildly nutty flavor. It has a good smoke point of 410°F, making it suitable for stir-frying and shallow-frying, but not deep-frying. Try it in dressings and marinades as well as for cooking eggs, poultry, and fish.

AT-A-GLANCE INFO

NUTRITIONAL HIGHLIGHT: Good source of oleic (Om-9) and vitamin E; richest source of palmitoleic acid

COUNTRY OF ORIGIN: Australia

STORAGE: Macadamia nut oil has a long shelf life of about 2 years. Best stored at room temperature as the oil may cloud if chilled—this does not affect the oil in any way and it can be easily restored by standing the bottle in warm water.

ALTERNATIVE: Hazelnut oil

RECOMMENDED: Try the brand Australian Macadamia Nut Oil.

FLAX SEED OIL

The flax plant, *Linum usitatissimum*, is cultivated for linen, and has been grown since Greek and Roman times. The seeds are used as a food grain in India, and in the Western world, the seeds are taken as a health supplement, chiefly as a bowel cleanser.

The small, brown, shiny, flattish seeds of the flax plant are also pressed to give an oil (also known as linseed oil), and this is an important ingredient in paints and varnishes, for which it is extracted—it is the traditional varnish for a cricket bat, for instance.

When cold pressed, flax seed oil is one of the richest sources of omega-3 essential fatty acids (linolenic acid). In nutritional terms flax oil is something of a "wonder oil," given that the metabolism converts the short chain omega-3 fatty acids into long chain fatty acids. The oil is clear and light golden yellow, with an oily, slightly sweet fragrance. It tastes slightly bittersweet, with a grainy/grassy flavor.

It is usually taken by the teaspoon as a health supplement or drizzled over fruit, yogurt, or cereal. It should not be heated, but could be made into a salad dressing, particularly when served with other toasted seeds and nuts.

AT-A-GLANCE INFO

NUTRITIONAL HIGHLIGHT: Rich source of linoleic acid (Om-3)

COUNTRY OF ORIGIN: various

STORAGE: Keep for 12 months unopened; once opened refrigerate and use within 6 months.

ALTERNATIVE: Hemp oil or mustard seed oil

RECOMMENDED: GranoVita Organic Flax Oil

WARNING: Not suitable for infants under 12 months old.

SESAME OIL

The sesame plant, *Sesamum indicum*, is an upright annual herb, which grows up to 6½ feet tall. It was one of the first oil-yielding plants to be cultivated by the ancient Egyptians, and the name is one of the few words to have passed into modern language from these times—the word "sesame" comes from the ancient Egyptian word *sesemt*. Wild species are African with one exception, which was introduced to India in very early times. Sesame has been mentioned throughout history and is recognized as one of the most important flavorings of southern Asian, Middle Eastern, and Oriental cookery.

The plant bears small, fat pods, which spring open when ripe, allowing the seeds to scatter— hence, every magician's favorite catchphrase: "Open Sesame!" The pods contain many small pear-shaped seeds, which may be white, yellow, brown, or black depending on

AT-A-GLANCE INFO

NUTRITIONAL HIGHLIGHT: Vitamin E; natural preservatives sesamol and sesamin

COUNTRY OF ORIGIN: various

STORAGE: shelf life of 12 months

ALTERNATIVE: Walnut oil

RECOMMENDED: Kadoya Sesame Oil, Bachun Fragrant Sesame Oil

WARNING: An allergy to sesame is one of the most common. It can lead to anaphylactic shock which can be fatal, and persons allergic to sesame seeds are usually allergic to sesame oil. Always consult your doctor for advice if you have a nut allergy before ingesting sesame oil.

Sesame oil and sesame seeds

the variety. Once they are hulled, the kernel inside is white. The seeds have a fragrant nutty flavor, which is developed further once the seeds have been roasted.

After hulling, the seeds are usually toasted, although oil from a cold pressing is made. This is almost colorless and only slightly nutty tasting. It is available in Western health stores. Asian sesame oil derives its dark color and flavor from toasted and hulled sesame seeds. It is richly nutty and fragrant and is commonly used in south Indian, Chinese, Japanese, and Korean cuisine, usually added at the end of cooking as a flavor highlight and not used as a cooking medium. Indian sesame oil, called gingelly or til oil, is golden and sweetly nutty because it is mixed with *jaggery*, a palm sugar. Refined sesame oil is very common in Europe and the US and it is also used in commercial margarine making. Many local Asian brands are graded in

degrees of hot-temperature pressing; some of the darkest varieties having a really burnt, bitter taste and are practically black in color.

Sesame oil is not an oil for cooking with. It is added at the end of cooking to add a nutty flavor to a finished dish. It can liven up plain rice, noodles, or mashed potatoes with just one or two teaspoonfuls. Drizzle over plain steamed fish, chicken, or vegetables to add an extra hint of flavor, and scatter with a few seeds for extra texture. You can use a teaspoon or so to flavor some of the neutral oils like peanut (see page 34) or sunflower (see page 74) for making marinades or mayonnaise—a ratio of 1 part sesame to 5 parts neutral oil offers a mild to medium nutty, savory flavor.

Sesame oil is also used as a massage oil as it is able to penetrate the skin easily, and it is believed to darken the hair when used as a scalp massage oil.

RAPESEED OIL

Rape, *Brassicus napus*, is one of the oldest members of the mustard or cabbage family. It is also known as oilseed rape, rapa, and rapaseed. Where it has been genetically cultivated, it is known as canola (see page 46). Rape is a widely grown crop and its bright yellow flowers are a familiar sight in fields in late spring/early summer months. It is grown for vegetable oil, animal feed, and bio-diesel across Europe, Canada, the US, Australia, China, and India. After soybean (see page 88) and palm oil (see page 90), it is the third largest vegetable oil crop.

The subspecies *B. oleifera* is the source of rapeseed oil most widely used in cooking. Natural rapeseed oil contains erucic acid and glucosinolates, which are mildly toxic to humans in large doses and have anti-nutritional properties. In the US and Canada, this has led to the development of a variety of rapeseed which has a low erucic acid content and this is used to make canola oil. The oilseed types that have been bred in Europe for food have been selected for their very low levels of this substance and are frequently checked to make sure they comply with levels within the accepted safety limit.

AT-A-GLANCE INFO

NUTRITIONAL HIGHLIGHT: Good source of oleic (Om-9) and linoleic acid (Om-6)

COUNTRY OF ORIGIN: various

STORAGE: Shelf life of about 12 months

ALTERNATIVE: Sunflower oil

RECOMMENDED: Try Borderfields Ltd Oleifera Extra Virgin Rapeseed Oil which is taken from the first pressing of the seed. It has a delicious rich flavor and is packaged in an elegant, slim bottle.

Rape crop field

The most common type of rapeseed oil on the supermarket shelves is a highly refined and processed oil with a bland flavor and light golden color. It is suitable for use as a general cooking oil.

Rapeseed is a heavy nectar producer and bees produce a light colored, distinct peppery honey from it. It is usually blended with other honeys to give a more palatable table product. However, this high-pollen producing crop is also believed to cause an allergic reaction to hay fever and asthma sufferers due to its vast production sites.

Rapeseed oil contains both omega-6 and omega-3 fatty acids in a ratio of 2 to 1 and is second only to flax seed oil in omega-3 fatty acids. It is one of the most heart-healthy oils and has been reported to reduce cholesterol levels, lower blood serum triglyceride levels, and keep blood platelets from sticking together.

More excitingly, some UK farmers have started to produce cold-pressed rapeseed oil as a product to compete with olive oil. A simple process produces cold-pressed rapeseed oil and no heat or additives are used. The product has a pleasantly subtle nutty flavor and is rich golden yellow in color. It is more expensive than the general rapeseed oil, but compares favorably to a good-quality olive oil.

Nutritionally, vitamins E and D can be found in cold-pressed rapeseed oil, as well as 59 percent monounsaturated and 30 percent polyunsaturated fatty acids. Cold-pressed rapeseed oil contains 6 percent saturated fat, where most olive oils and sunflower oils have about 13 percent. Use this oil wherever you would use olive oil. It has a high smoke point of approx 450°F so it will cook safely at high temperatures. It makes delicious roasted root vegetables and is good for stir-fries. For a special mayonnaise, cold-pressed rapeseed oil is subtle enough to use on its own and gives a golden hue to the finished dressing. It is also good for cake baking.

CANOLA OIL

This is an edible oil derived in Canada in the 1970s. It is a trademarked quality description of a group of cultivars of rapeseed variants from which low erucic acid rapeseed oil and low glucosinolate meal are obtained. The word "canola" was derived from "CANadian Oil, Low Acid" in 1978. Its other name, "lear," comes from the words "Low Erucic Acid Rapeseed." Canola was developed through conventional plant breeding from rapeseed, an oilseed plant with roots in ancient civilization (see separate entry for rapeseed oil, page 44). The negative associations with the word "rape" in North America resulted in the more marketing-friendly name "canola." The change in name also serves to distinguish it from regular rapeseed oil, which has a much higher erucic acid content.

Canola was once a specialty crop, but now it is a huge commercial export. Canada and the US produce between 7.8 and 11.2 million tons of seed per year and customers include Japan, Mexico, China, and Pakistan. The bulk of canola oil goes to the US, with smaller amounts shipped to Taiwan, Mexico, China, and Europe. Canola is also grown in Australia.

Hundreds of years ago, rapeseed oil was only used as a lamp oil in parts of Asia and Europe. As time progressed, people began cooking with it. Once steam power was

AT-A-GLANCE INFO

NUTRITIONAL HIGHLIGHT: Good source of oleic (Om-9) and linoleic acid (Om-6)

COUNTRY OF ORIGIN: Canada

STORAGE: Shelf life of about 12 months

ALTERNATIVE: Sunflower oil, any vegetable oil

RECOMMENDED: Try Mazola Canola Oil or Crisco Pure Canola Oil (www.plumgoodfood.com).

invented, commercial uses for the oil were employed such as lubrication for steam-driven vessels and machinery. World War II saw high demand for the oil and when the war blocked European and Asian sources of rapeseed oil, a critical shortage developed and Canada began to expand its limited rapeseed production. After the war, demand declined, so farmers began to look for other uses for the plant and its products. However, rapeseed oil at this time had a distinctive taste and a disagreeable greenish color due to the presence of chlorophyll. It also contained a high concentration of erucic acid—today levels of erucic acid in human foods are restricted in the US, due to the concerns that it may adversely affect the heart. Even as a feed meal it was not particularly appealing to livestock, due to high levels of sharp-tasting compounds called glucosinolates.

Plant breeders in Canada began working to improve the quality of the plant, and by 1974 a variety was produced which was low in both erucic acid and glucosinolates; it was named canola. Due to advances in genetic modification, a variety has now been developed which is considered to be the most disease and drought-resistant variety of canola to date.

Canola oil contains little or no saturated fat and has a high (60 percent) monounsaturated oil content and a good omega-3 fatty acids profile. The Canola Council of Canada states that it is completely safe and is the healthiest of all commonly used cooking oils. Traditional rapeseed oil contains higher amounts of erucic acid and glucosinolates, both of which were deemed undesirable for human consumption by the United States Food and Drug Administration (USFDA). Canola oil contains only 0.5 to 1 percent erucic acid, well below the 2 percent limit set by the USFDA.

Canola oil is clear and pale golden in color with a very mild, fresh flavor. It can be used interchangeably with any vegetable oil in baking, shallow-, and deep-frying, and as a salad dressing oil. It imparts little or no flavor of its own so is a good choice when other food flavors are to be preserved. It has a good shelf life and is a stable oil. Apart from use in the kitchen, canola oil is being developed as a possible source for manufacturing bio-diesel.

Oil-popped popcorn

POPPY SEED OIL

Poppy seed oil is obtained from the tiny seeds of the opium poppy, *Papaver somniferum*, native to Mediterranean regions, India, China, Turkey, and Central Asia. The seeds are edible and non-toxic and the oil has no narcotic properties, since the fluid in the bud that becomes opium is not present once the seeds are fully formed. The seeds have been used in cooking for thousands of years and were highly prized by the ancient Greeks for their health-giving properties. The oil is made in parts of Europe and India, and is highly esteemed, especially in northern France where is it known as "huile blanche."

Raw, cold-pressed poppy seed oil has the best flavor, is slightly nutty, and has a smooth, silky texture. It is light golden in color. More refined poppy seed oils are practically colorless, with little aroma or flavor.

As with all raw, cold-pressed oils, poppy seed oil is not suitable for cooking but should be used as a finishing oil or a dipping oil for fresh bread. Use with simple flavors to enjoy the subtle taste at its best. Try drizzling over salads and freshly cooked vegetables, or toss into noodles along with some lightly toasted whole poppy seeds for extra nuttiness.

Poppy seed oil is also used as a moisturizer in balms and soaps, and as a conditioner for the hair.

AT-A-GLANCE INFO

NUTRITIONAL HIGHLIGHT: Good source of linoleic acid (Om-6)

COUNTRY OF ORIGIN: Europe and India

STORAGE: Raw poppy seed oil should be refrigerated in accordance to the manufacturer's instructions.

ALTERNATIVE: 1 part almond oil or 1 part hazelnut oil to 2 parts sunflower oil

RECOMMENDED: Try Rejuvantive Foods 100% Organic Poppy Seed Oil.

TEA SEED OIL

Because tea plants are grown for their leaves and are constantly pruned, this discourages the formation of seeds. Certain varieties, however, are allowed to produce seeds for the extraction of an oil, which is very similar to olive oil. Tea seed oil is cold pressed mainly from the seeds of *Camellia oleifera* but also from *C. sinensis*, *C. japonica*, and *C. sasanqua*. These varieties are grown in the tropical rainforest and humid subtropical areas of China, Assam, and North Vietnam.

Tea seeds are contained in capsules. Inside the shiny dark brown seed coat lies an oil-rich kernel. When the fruits are mature they fall to the ground and are gathered and then dried in the sun. The outer husks are removed by hand and the kernels ground to produce a fine meal. The oil is either extracted by pressing or by solvent extraction.

Tea seed oil resembles olive oil and grapeseed oil. It is pale amber-green in color with a sweet, herbal aroma. It has a high smoke point of 485°F and is the main cooking oil in some parts of southern China. It is used in marinades and sauces as well as for frying and stir-fries. It is a very stable oil and keeps well. In addition to domestic use, it is used in margarine production, and the manufacture of soap, hair oil, lubricants, paint, and a rust-proofing oil. Japanese tea seed oil is used for setting the hair of Sumo wrestlers and for the traditional deep-fried dish, *tempura*.

AT-A-GLANCE INFO

NUTRITIONAL HIGHLIGHT: Good source of oleic acid (Om-9)

COUNTRY OF ORIGIN: China, North Vietnam

STORAGE: Shelf life of 12 to 18 months

ALTERNATIVE: Grapeseed oil

RECOMMENDED: Try Cold Pressed Extra Virgin Tea Seed Oil.

PUMPKIN SEED OIL

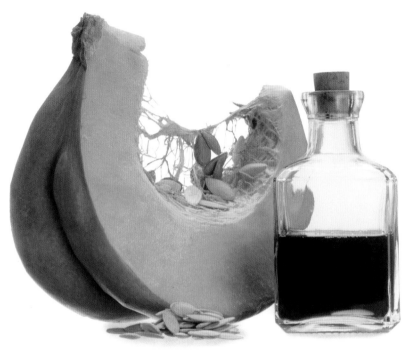

This oil originates from the large vegetable fruit—typically orange, round, and ribbed—the *Cucurbita pepo* or field pumpkin.

Pumpkin seed oil is a specialty of Steiermark, or the Austrian province of Styria, located in the south-eastern corner of Austria which borders Hungary, Slovenia, and Italy. Styria's cuisine has, therefore, been greatly influenced by both eastern and western cultures, and pumpkin seed oil is part of the traditional culinary history.

The oil is dark green-brown and has a toasty aroma. The flavor is rich and nutty. Use pumpkin seed oil like sesame seed oil, not for cooking, but as a flavoring or condiment. The strong color and flavor of pumpkin seed oil makes it ideal for use as a stand alone salad dressing, for bread dipping, and for drizzling over finished dishes— use it with roasted meats, fish, or vegetables. It is particularly good drizzled over barbecued food and other robust dishes. For a hint of the rich flavor of pumpkin, try diluting it with 4 parts peanut (see page 34) or grapeseed oil (see page 33) to 1 part pumpkin seed, and use as a delicious base for mayonnaise.

This unusual oil has a high content of unsaturated fats, linoleic, and oleic acids, as well as beta-carotene, vitamin E, and zinc.

AT-A-GLANCE INFO

NUTRITIONAL HIGHLIGHT: Good source of oleic (Om-9) and linoleic acid (Om-6) along with vitamin E and zinc

COUNTRY OF ORIGIN: Austria

STORAGE: Shelf life of about 12 months

ALTERNATIVE: Walnut oil or sesame seed oil

RECOMMENDED: Try Merchant Gourmet Austrian Roasted Pumpkin Seed Oil.

HEMP (SEED) OIL

An oil pressed from the seeds of the infamous plant *Cannabis sativa*. The plant is cultivated as a source of fiber for rope-making and illegally for various narcotic substances. The edible seeds are not narcotic and are now widely renowned as a source of a complete combination of fatty acids.

Refined hemp oil is clear with little flavor. It is widely used in body care products, lubricants, paints, and industrial uses. Antimicrobial properties make it a useful ingredient for soaps, shampoos, and detergents. The cold-pressed, unrefined hemp oil is light green, with a mild, nutty, grassy aroma and flavor. This type of hemp oil is taken for its health benefits. The oil is of high nutritional value because its 3 to 1 ratio of omega-6 to omega-3 essential fatty acids (EFAs) matches the balance required by the human body. It should not be heated as this will destroy the EFAs and can result in the production of unhealthy trans-fatty acids and increased peroxide values. It is best added to foods once removed from direct heat to improve both their flavor and nutritional content. It can be taken by the teaspoon as a health supplement—see bottle label for directions—or drizzled over salads, yogurt, or fruit, or whizzed up in a smoothie.

AT-A-GLANCE INFO

NUTRITIONAL HIGHLIGHT: A complete source of EFAs

COUNTRY OF ORIGIN: various

STORAGE: Hemp oil has a shelf life of about 12 months—keep away from direct sunlight. Keep bottles tightly sealed after opening and store in the refrigerator or freezer for up to 6 weeks.

ALTERNATIVE: Flax seed oil

RECOMMENDED: GranoVita Organic Hemp Oil

KUSUM OIL

KAPOK SEED OIL

The smooth loofah, *Luffa cylindrical*, is a member of the gourd family. It grows in tropical Asia and China as well as Brazil and the Caribbean, and can tolerate a wide range of climatic and soil conditions. The fruits grow on an attractive vine and resemble a long cucumber with deep, regular furrows on the surface. It is also known as the "sponge" or "dish cloth" gourd.

Young loofahs are eaten mostly in China and the Caribbean as a vegetable. When they age they become too fibrous to be eaten, so they are dried, peeled, and made into the familiar abrasive bath sponges. During this process, the black seeds are removed from the internal tissue; they contain about 40 percent oil and are used to produce an edible oil, which is rich in linoleic acid.

This oil is obtained from the seeds of the kapok or silk cotton tree (see facing page), part of the *Bombax* genus of primarily tropical trees in the mallow family. They are native to tropical areas in West Africa, the Indian subcontinent, South-east Asia, as well as sub-tropical regions of eastern Asia and northern Australia. The most well known species is *B. ceiba*, which is widely cultivated throughout tropical and sub-tropcial regions of the world. *Bombax* species are among the largest trees in their regions, reaching 98 to 130 feet high. They bear long red flowers between January and March before the leaves develop. The "fruit" forms into a husk containing seeds covered by a fiber similar to that of cotton, though with shorter fibers than cotton—it does not lend itself to textile production but is a useful stuffing material.

The seeds are a by-product and are pressed to yield an edible oil which is produced in India, Indonesia, and Malaysia. Kapok oil is the most sensitive of all the vegetable oils and becomes rancid quickly when exposed to air. It has a yellow color and a pleasant, mild odor and taste. It has similar characteristics to cotton seed oil (see page 57). It is used locally as a cooking oil, and also in soap production and for lubrication.

AT-A-GLANCE INFO

NUTRITIONAL HIGHLIGHT: Good source of Linoleic acid (Om-6)

COUNTRY OF ORIGIN: Tropical Asia and Brazil

ALTERNATIVE: Any nut or seed oil

RECOMMENDED: Not widely available—local use only

AT-A-GLANCE INFO

NUTRITIONAL HIGHLIGHT: Good source of Linoleic acid (Om-6)

COUNTRY OF ORIGIN: India, Indonesia and Malaysia

ALTERNATIVE: Sunflower oil

RECOMMENDED: Not widely available—local or commercial use only

AVOCADO OIL

The avocado tree, *Persea gratissima*, is native to central and southern America. Now widely distributed in tropical and subtropical countries worldwide and warmer areas of southern Europe, the principle growers are Mexico, the US, Brazil, the Dominican Republic, and Israel.

The avocado tree grows to a height of 65 feet and starts to bear fruit when it reaches 3 to 6 years old. The well-known single-seeded avocado fruit with its familiar leathery skin ranges in color from yellow-green to purple depending on the variety. The edible pulp is yellowy-green and has a buttery consistency. The pulp contains between 3 and 30 percent oil, and as the fruit ripens, the oil content increases. In South Africa, fruit is picked for fresh consumption when the oil content is about 8 percent but at this stage of ripeness it is not suitable for oil extraction. Oil is generally extracted from avocados that are left to fully ripen after harvesting.

The avocado fruits are usually hand picked and then allowed to ripen fully to give maximum oil yield. Depending on the method to be used for oil extraction the fruit may then be opened and, after removing the seed,

---

AT-A-GLANCE INFO

NUTRITIONAL HIGHLIGHT: Good source of Oleic acid (Om-9)

COUNTRY OF ORIGIN: New Zealand

STORAGE: Usually sold in dark glass bottles to protect the nutritional content, it is best stored out of the light and will keep for about 2 years.

ALTERNATIVE: Extra Virgin Olive oil

RECOMMENDED: New Zealand Olivado Avocado Oil for a smooth, mild fruity flavor

sun dried. One method involves mashing the pulp and, after boiling, skimming off the oil. Other methods include high pressure pressing of dried slices, solvent extraction, expellers, presses, and centrifugal extraction. The crude oil is dark green/brown in color, red under reflected light due to its high chlorophyll content, and this makes it very unstable. It can degrade very quickly, so after extraction of oil for culinary use it is stabilized in order to give it a longer shelf life.

Nutritionally speaking, avocado oil is very rich in protein, lecithin, and vitamins A, B and D, and contains high levels of oleic acid (64 percent). The oil is monosaturated and contains beta-sitosterols, which act to reduce bad cholesterol in the body, and at the same time, increase good cholesterol.

In the cosmetic industry, avocado oil is used in the production of hair care products, face and hand creams, and for sunscreen lotions. After it is refined, it is suitable for culinary use and is rapidly becoming one of the gourmet "must have" oils for the modern kitchen. The oil is green like olive oil and has a rich, delicate, buttery avocado flavor. You can use it for cooking like olive oil and it is particularly good with fish and chicken. It makes a delicious dressing for pasta. Drizzle over fresh avocados to enhance their flavor, or serve as an indulgent appetizer and for bread dipping.

Avocado and cherry tomato salad drizzled with avocado oil

DIKA NUT OIL

COTTON SEED OIL

The nut, kernel, or seed of the mango-like fruit of the *Irvingia gabonensis*, a wild tree of West Africa, particularly Gabon, is also known by the common names wild mango, African mango, or bush mango. The nuts, which resemble peanuts, called *agbono* or *apon*, are oily and are eaten on their own whole, or are ground and used in cooking. They are subtly aromatic and have a high content of mucilage, which enables them to be used as a thickening agent for dishes such as *agbono* soup. Once ground, the product is called dika bread or Gabon chocolate—this is sometimes spiced, and the paste can also be smoked. The paste is used as a flavoring for fish, meat, and plantain dishes.

The paste can be heated to yield an oil or butter, which is reminiscent of cocoa butter, and the nuts may also be pressed for a locally-used crude vegetable oil.

As a plant, cotton, *Gossypium barbadernse*, has been around since the time of the earliest ancient civilizations, and its fibrous tufts have been used in the cloth trade for centuries. Up until the end of the 19th century, the seeds of the plant were discarded once the fibers had been removed, but once it was discovered that cotton seeds could be pressed to produce oil, the oil became an important by-product of the cloth industry. Cotton is grown widely in the US, India, Sudan, Egypt, and Brazil.

After pressing, the oil is dark and requires refinement in order to render it edible. The refined oil is clear and very pale golden in color (see facing page). It is light to pour and flavorless. It must be used fresh, as it goes rancid quickly once it is exposed to the air, and so it is mainly used commercially in the manufacture of margarines and cooking fats. Locally, it is used fresh as a cooking oil or dressing. Cotton seed oil is also used in soaps, for nail polish remover and in various creams, particularly those for sensitive skin, such as baby care creams.

AT-A-GLANCE INFO

NUTRITIONAL HIGHLIGHT: High in saturated fatty acids

COUNTRY OF ORIGIN: West Africa

STORAGE: It has poor storage capabilities so is usually used fresh

ALTERNATIVE: Shea butter or coconut butter

RECOMMENDED: Used locally only

AT-A-GLANCE INFO

NUTRITIONAL HIGHLIGHT: Good source of Linoleic acid (Om-6)

COUNTRY OF ORIGIN: various

STORAGE: It has poor storage capabilities so is usually used fresh

RECOMMENDED: Plainsmen Cottonseed cooking oil and salad oil

OLIVE OIL

Selección especial Carbonell

Regarded by many as the original oil, the oil from the olive tree, *Olea europaea*, and its fruit date back to prehistoric times. The tree is native to the Mediterranean region, and to this day, this is where the bulk of olive oil comes from. The English word "oil," Italian "olio," and French "huile" are all derived from the ancient Greek word for olive, *elaia*. The tree is highly prized in literature and is mentioned in the Bible, ancient Greek and Roman texts, and Shakespeare; it has been painted by some of the world's greatest masters of art, and in culinary circles, it is second to none for its fine flavor and color, and to many it symbolizes a true taste of the Mediterranean.

Olive oil is unique amongst oils for the fact that the oil is pressed from the fruit flesh rather than a grain, seed, or nut, which means that it retains the fruity flavor and color of the original olive fruit. The olive tree is evergreen with thin silvery-green leaves. It has deep roots,

AT-A-GLANCE INFO

NUTRITIONAL HIGHLIGHT: Good source of oleic acid (Om-9)

COUNTRY OF ORIGIN: Various

STORAGE: Best bought in small quantities. Store in a cool, dark place and, after opening, use within a month or 2. Always check manufacturer's instructions. For more information, see main text.

ALTERNATIVE: Avocado oil

RECOMMENDED: See page 62

L'Olio Lizzanello Ginni Calogiuri

Carapelli Firenze

and and is slow to mature, but lives for many years. The tree prefers sunny climes as it isn't able to withstand frost. It is the distinctive olive tree groves on many a hillside or meadow plane in the Mediterranean area that shape the landscape and define the region. The fruit of the tree form smallish green fleshy drupes, which hang singly off a short stalk. The flesh has a high oil content (up to 30 percent) and also a glucoside, which gives it a bitterness—especially pronounced in unripe fruit. Removing this flavor is the first stage of the process when preparing table olives, but during the pressing stage for oil making, the glucoside separates out naturally.

There are many varieties of olives; not all are used to make olive oil, but 90 percent of the olives grown in the world are used to make oil. Different countries grow different varieties to suit the local conditions and environment. As a general rule, Italian olive oil is made with more than 1 variety of olive (Italians grow about

50 different types of olive for oil alone), whilst other countries tend to use a single variety. The main producers of olive oil are Spain, Italy, Greece, Tunisia, and Turkey. Other producers of note include Portugal, Morocco, the US, Israel, Australia, the Lebanon, and Argentina. France, although widely associated with the oil through its cooking, is quite a minor producer on the global scale. Spain is undoubtedly the world's number 1 producer of olive oil, and Andalusia is the largest producing region. The *Picual* olive is the most widely used variety in Spain, although its name gets changed slightly in different regions. This olive gives a very stable oil with an aromatic fruity flavor and a distinct bitter note. Other varieties include: the *Cornicabra* olive which gives a very fruity and aromatic oil, with a pungent note and stable quality; *Hojiblanca* olive oil is mildly pungent, less fruity, aromatic with a lower stability; and the oil from the *Arbequina* olive is full of ripe, fruity flavor. It is

Filippo Berio Mild and Light Oil

Filippo Berio Gusto Fruttato

very fragrant, with a medium to low stability, and is a less bitter oil than other varieties. Other factors such as soil, topology, crop maintenance, irrigation, and harvesting technique all affect the quality of the oil produced.

The essential elements of olive oil production have remained unchanged for centuries. Whilst machinery and equipment have advanced and factory methods have developed, the basic processes have stayed the same. Olives for oil must be quite ripe, and in the Mediterranean regions, harvesting takes place from late fall and continues into the winter months. Getting the correct level of ripeness is the most critical part of olive oil making. The ultimate flavor of the finished product is determined by the ripeness of the fruit when it goes to be pressed. Olives start life as small, bright-green hard fruits and as they develop they plump out and become fleshier, and change color to yellow-green, pinkish to purple, and finally black. Unripe green olives have a herby, fresh and bitter flavor but keep very well, whilst riper fruit have a more characteristic olive flavor. By the time they are fully ripe, the flesh takes on a buttery flavor

that is not very fruity and stores poorly. There is usually a window of 2 to 3 weeks for the optimum harvest time when the olives reach their best quality for oil making.

The olives are usually hand picked, although mechanical tree-shakers are also used. They are then gathered, undamaged, ready for crushing. The olives are pressed on fibrous mats, without breaking the stones, and the oil and a bitter watery liquid drains off into a collecting vessel. Once the 2 substances are allowed to separate from each other, the water is siphoned off for farm use. The oil is then filtered to varying degrees. The most prized olive oil is completely unfiltered. It is bottled as soon as possible after the first pressing and offers a very fresh-tasting fruity flavor, with subtle notes that are often undetectable in more filtered products. It is very green, but in time the brightness fades. It will also contain a characteristic cloudy vegetable residue called *fondo*, which is completely harmless and perfectly edible—a simple shake of the bottle before use will help distribute it in the oil and stop it collecting at the bottom only to be wasted. This oil is usually enjoyed by the

OLIVE OIL

local community of olive pickers around harvest time because it doesn't keep well—it is a fine reward for all their hard work.

Olive oil is classified for marketing purposes under regulations set out by the headquarters of the International Olive Oil Council in Madrid. For an oil to be labeled "virgin" it must be made solely from the fruit of the olive tree and the oil should be made by methods that do not lead to it being adulterated in any way. In the US, "virgin" oil is oil from the first pressing of olives that is suitable for human consumption without undergoing further processing. Oils are graded according to the level of oleic acid, the best quality oils having the lowest acidity levels (and highest prices):

Cold-pressed extra virgin—has to have an acidity of less than or equal to 1 percent and be subjected to heat less than 86°F during processing. This oil can either be filtered to give a clear, bright oil, or unfiltered, with vegetable residue remaining in the oil.

Virgin (fine)—lower or equal to 2 percent oleic acid.

Virgin (semi-fine or ordinary)—lower or equal to 3.3 percent.

Within this classification, the finished oil can be a blend of oils from different groves and olive varieties, in order to produce a consistently top quality product. Or, like fine wine, they can be made from olives borne of a single estate and of a single olive variety. As with a vineyard, the quality of the olive harvest can vary from year to year and thus affect the oil produced. These single estate oils are quite costly, and like a good balsamic vinegar, are best saved for fine dressings or as a table or dipping condiment. As well as the aforementioned qualities, the different grades of oil must have a fine taste and aroma. The variation of flavor between oils can be extreme; some are seemingly pungent and peppery, whilst others are rich and fruity.

Filippo Berio Gusto Fruttato

The biggest brand label producers like Filippo Berio from Italy and Carbonell from Spain have experienced and skilful blenders who produce consistent, excellent products for the general market, each with its own unique, yet unchanging, flavor.

Olive oil that isn't suitable for the above grading is usually refined in some way. The leftover pulp from the first pressing is then subject to further extraction to squeeze out every last drop of oil. Refined olive oil is obtained from virgin olive oil using methods that do not change its structure. Standard olive oil is a mix of refined oil and virgin oil fit for human consumption. By the time the oil has reached the last classification it is a fraction of its former self in terms of flavor, and is really aimed at the general cooking oil market. As is the norm, when it comes to quality, you get what you pay for. Any oil labeled simply as "olive oil" will be cheap and probably not very tasty. When choosing an oil, it is always worth checking the label for an indication of a region of origin or a clear identification as to where the olives have been grown and pressed.

QUALITY OLIVE OIL PRODUCERS AROUND THE WORLD

Listed below are some quality olive oil producers from different countries that you might like to look out for and try:

SPAIN

Dauro de L'Epoda

- Dauro de L'Epoda—extra virgin unfiltered olive oil, paler in color with a distinct olive aroma and slightly sweet, fruity flavor.

- Nunez de Prado—organic, unfiltered extra virgin oil, which is bottled within three hours of picking. It is a "free run" oil, which comes from the crushing of the fruit before it is pressed. This is a very fresh and flowery oil with rich aromas and a peppery edge to its flavor. Each bottle is individually numbered and sealed by hand.

- Valderrama—single estate, cold pressed, and unfiltered extra virgin oil pressed within 45 minutes of picking. It has a smooth, light peppery taste, and a mild, fragrant aroma.

ITALY

Valderrama Estate

- Badia a Coltibuono's Albereto—an unfiltered organic extra virgin olive oil, rich emerald-green in color, from this famous Tuscan estate. The oil is intensely aromatic and herbal, with a slight bitter-leaf note. Each bottle is numbered and the neck tag provides the information necessary to research its production.

- Frescobaldi Laudemio—regarded as one of the world's best oils, produced on the Frescobaldi wine estates in Tuscany. This extra virgin single estate oil is made from Frantoio, Maraiolio, and Leccino olives. It is a fresh green color and has a herbal, sweet fresh flavor. It is expensive but makes a real difference to a leaf salad.

- Gianni Calogiuzi—makes an extra virgin olive oil called "Lizzanello" named after the place in Puglia where the olive trees grow and the oil is made. Rich golden yellow/green in color, its flavor is creamy smooth and fruity. Perfect as a dipping oil.

GREECE

- Biolea—an organic extra virgin oil made from Koroneiki olives grown on the Astrikas estate in North-west Crete. The Dimitriadis family have been producing oil on this estate since the mid-18th century. The oil has rich herbal aromas and flavors with a peppery kick.

- Ionis Kalamantra—extra virgin olive oil made from the Koroneiki olive, the most renowned Greek variety. Yellow-green in color, this oil is smooth in texture but has a robust, peppery note. It is ideal as a salad dressing.

Ionis Kalamatra

FRANCE

- Aliziari—a single estate extra virgin oil produced from olives on the hills behind the Cote d'Azur. The oil is typically Provencal in style—fresh, fruity, and sweet but with a hint of nutty spice. The oil is packaged in a distinctive and attractive tin.

- A l'Olivier—an extra virgin oil from Provence with a sweet, fragrant taste, milder than Italian varieties. It is sold in a quaint Parisian shop, founded in 1822, from a stone crock which helps preserve its freshness.

SOUTH AFRICA

- Morgenster—regarded as one of the best oil producers of South Africa. This single estate oil from South Africa uses old Italian varieties of olive and has a sweet, fruity flavor with a delicate peppery note.

- So! Gourmet—cold-pressed extra virgin olive oil from South Africa, packaged in a trendy, small frosted glass bottle, it is yellow-green in color and light, fruity, and fresh in flavor. Best poured over salads and vegetables.

NORTH AMERICA

- Napa Valley Special Reserve—extra virgin oil from California. Deep

Cobram Estate

green with an earthy, nutty flavor and peppery finish, it is grown fertilizer- and pesticide- free. The olive trees were planted in the early 19th century.

AUSTRALIA

- Cobram Estate Murray Valley—an extra virgin olive oil from Australia which has won several awards. It is richly green in color with a fresh, fruity flavor and slightly peppery aftertaste. Ideal for dressing pasta, soups, and risottos.

NEW ZEALAND

- Serendipity—a single estate oil from Marlborough, New Zealand. It is extra virgin, and is pressed and bottled on site. It has a greenish-gold color and fruity/herbal flavor with a peppery note.

So! Gourmet

Extra virgin olive oil with balsamic vinegar and fresh Italian bread

No other naturally produced oil has as large an amount of monounsaturated fat as olive oil. Furthermore, the modest amount of well-balanced polyunsaturated fatty acids and vitamin E means that it is well-protected by its own natural antioxidant substances. Its primary fatty acids are monounsaturated oleic acid (about 75 percent) and poly-unsaturated linoleic acid (about 8 percent). This combination of fatty acids means that olive oil has an excellent capacity for controlling and maintaining levels of cholesterol in the blood. The color of olive oil is dependent on the pigments in the fruit—green olives give a green oil because of the high chlorophyll content and other antioxidant polyphenols that are present. Extra virgin olive oil, from the first pressing of the olives, contains higher levels of antioxidants, particularly vitamin E and phenols, because it is less processed. Olive oil is the second best natural source of vitamin K available—an important factor in blood clotting. This is associated with chlorophyll in as much as to say that the greener the oil (or vegetable), the more vitamin K that is present.

When it comes to eating olive oil and using it in your kitchen, it comes down to personal taste. If you want the health benefits and good fruity olive flavor, you would be best to use a good-quality extra virgin oil and use it straight, drizzled over salads, fresh pasta, to dress vegetables, broiled fish, or chicken. You can use it as an antipasto dip for fresh crusty bread—traditionally partnered with a good-quality balsamic vinegar, it makes a winning combination. Try spooning a little on top of a freshly-made sweet tomato soup for a peppery, fruity kick. Where you don't want to overpower a dish, either use a less-flavored oil or blend the extra virgin with some plainer vegetable oil like sunflower (see page 74) or grapeseed (see page 33). The olive oil will help maintain the green color. For example, a mayonnaise made with all extra virgin oil would not only be expensive but quite overpowering when served as an accompaniment, so "watering" it down is a good option in this instance. For frying, it would be too costly for most people to use their prized single estate bottled oil for everyday cooking, so you may want to investigate a blended product.

Unlike wine, olive oil does not improve with age and once opened it will begin to slowly deteriorate. Heat, light, and air all speed up the deterioration of flavor, color, and nutrients, so avoid the temptation of buying your oil in large quantities unless you plan to get through it very quickly.

COCONUT OIL

Coconut oil is a tropical oil with many applications. It is usually extracted from copra (derived from the Malayalan word "kopra," meaning dried coconut). The world's largest exporter of the oil is the Philippines, and it has been a commercial product since the mid-19th century. There are different types of coconut oil, so it is worth checking the label when you buy a product. The state of the product you buy will depend on whether you live in a tropical or cooler climate. In a warm temperature zone, coconut oil will be in liquid form; below 76°F it will be solid and is often referred to as coconut butter.

True virgin coconut oil is a premium product. It is unrefined, produced without chemicals, and non-deodorized. The products of virgin coconut oil have a fresh coconut aroma and a mild coconut flavor. This oil can be used as a replacement for any oil in cooking.

AT-A-GLANCE INFO

NUTRITIONAL HIGHLIGHT: High saturated fat content

COUNTRY OF ORIGIN: Philippines, Malaysia, and Australia

STORAGE: Among the most stable of all oils, lasting up to 2 years due to its high saturated fat content. It is best stored in solid form, below 76 °F in order to extend its shelf life.

ALTERNATIVE: For flavor sunflower oil mixed with grated block or creamed coconut; for cooking, other vegetable oils.

RECOMMENDED: Try Virgin Coconut Oil from Coconut Connections.

COCONUT OIL

Coconut palm tree

Coconut oil is most commonly used in cooking, especially for frying, as it has a high smoke point, which makes it good for this purpose. In communities where coconut oil is widely used in cooking, the refined oil is the one most commonly used. Commercially, coconut oil is used extensively in making margarine, soap, and cosmetics. Hydrogenated or partially hydrogenated coconut oil is often used in non-dairy creamers and snack foods. Fractionated coconut oil is also used in the manufacture of essences, massage oils, and cosmetics. It makes an excellent skin moisturizer and softener. In India and Sri Lanka, coconut oil is commonly used for styling hair, and cooling or soothing the head. People of coastal Indian regions bathe in warm water after applying coconut oil all over the body and leaving it to soak in for an hour to keep body, skin, and hair healthy. Coconut oil is also used as a fuel for lamps and is currently used as a fuel for transportation and electricity generation in the Philippines and India.

In the kitchen, coconut oil can be used instead of other oils, butter, and cooking fats for frying (deep or shallow), broiling, and roasting. You can bake with it as a substitute for hard fat in a recipe—use $3/4$ the amount of coconut oil as you would use hard fat. It makes an ideal base oil for a curry, especially if you add coconut milk, or a stir-fry or noodle dish. Virgin coconut oils can be used to enrich ice creams or even as a spread on crackers or toasted bread as a butter or margarine replacement.

RICE BRAN OIL

Rice bran is a by-product of the pearling process of rice, *Oryza sativa*. It is extracted from the germ and inner husk of the rice, and contains 20 percent oil. It is a popular oil in Japan and China, where it is valued for deep-frying as it has a very high smoke point of 489°F.

Refined low-acid rice bran oil is pale yellow in color and very similar to corn (see page 93) and cotton seed oil (see page 57). It has a mild, clean flavor making it a good choice as a neutral oil for all types of cooking.

Rice bran oil contains a range of fats, with 47 percent of its fats monounsaturated, 33 percent polyunsaturated, and about 20 percent saturated. It is also rich in both vitamin E and oryzanol, an antioxidant that may help prevent heart attacks, and phytosterols—compounds believed to help lower cholesterol absorption.

Used in salad dressings, rice bran oil emulsifies well and complements gourmet vinegars because of its delicate flavor. Because it has such a light flavor, it is often used in baking. Try using rice bran oil in chocolate brownies for a nice light texture. It is also useful for coating baking sheets and cake pans. In Japan, rice bran oil has been used throughout history in soaps and skincare products.

AT-A-GLANCE INFO

NUTRITIONAL HIGHLIGHT: Good source of oleic (Om-9) and linoleic acid (Om-6), as well as vitamin E

COUNTRY OF ORIGIN: New Zealand

STORAGE: Store in a cool dark place. It has a long shelf life of about 2 years.

ALTERNATIVE: Sunflower oil, corn oil or cotton seed oil

RECOMMENDED: Alfa One Rice Bran Oil

BOTTLE GOURD OIL

The climbing plant, *Lagenaria siceraria*, is native to Africa, but has been cultivated in Asia and South America since prehistoric times. Today, it is widely cultivated throughout the tropical regions of the world such as India, Sri Lanka, Indonesia, Malaysia, the Philippines, China, Hong Kong, tropical Africa, Colombia, and Brazil.

The immature fruit is cooked and used as a vegetable. The peeled flesh is boiled, steamed, fried, and used in curries or made into fritters, particularly in African and Asian cuisine. The flesh is also dried for use out of season. The pulp around the seeds is a purgative and should not be eaten. The flesh of the mature fruit is dry, bitter, and inedible. Older gourds are scooped out and the skin shell is used as a container, or in some cases, fishing floats and musical instruments. Leaves and young shoots are cooked and used as a potherb.

Bottle gourd seeds are rich in oil. They are cooked and made into a vegetable curd similar to tofu. An edible oil is also obtained from the seed. It is used locally for cooking. The oil is similar to other gourd seed oils both in its composition of fatty acids (high in content of essential fatty acids, especially linoleic acid), and in the composition of its sterolic compounds, particularly spinasterol, which helps with the dispersion of cholesterol around the body.

AT-A-GLANCE INFO

NUTRITIONAL HIGHLIGHT: Good source of linoleic acid (Om-6)

COUNTRY OF ORIGIN: Various

ALTERNATIVE: Any nut or seed oil

RECOMMENDED: Not widely available—local use only at present

PILI NUT OIL

The fruit of the tree *Canarium ovatum* is from a family of around 600 species. It is native to the Philippines where it grows wild. It is an attractive evergreen tree with a resinous wood. It grows to about 65 feet in height and flowers frequently. The tree begins to bear fruits ready for harvest when it is between 7 and 10 years old. The fruit is almond-shaped, slender, and pointed (see facing page). The thin, oily green pulp inside it contains a triangular-shaped seed. The flesh is bittersweet in flavor and is a local delicacy, frequently served as a dessert, or accompanied by fish oil or sugar for dipping. The seed has a thick shell, which is hard to crack, and inside is the oil-bearing kernel with a high fat content of about 70 percent.

The oil is extracted when the nuts are fully mature. The fruits are knocked or shaken from the tree and then gathered from the ground. The shell is split with a machete-like tool called a *bolo*. The pili nut flesh is tender when fresh, with a taste that is a blend between a macadamia nut and a sweet pecan.

The delicately flavored light yellow oil is extracted when the nuts are fully mature, and is used for cooking in areas where coconuts are scarce. It is said to be very good as a baking product and for confectionery. The flavor resembles a cross between macadamia nut and Brazil nut oil. It is hoped that pili nut oil could be a major export in the future for its health benefits.

AT-A-GLANCE INFO

NUTRITIONAL HIGHLIGHT: Good source of oleic acid (Om-9); also palmitic acid (saturated)

COUNTRY OF ORIGIN: Philippines

ALTERNATIVE: Macadamia nut and Brazil nut oil

RECOMMENDED: Not widely available—local use only at present

PERILLA OIL

Perilla is a perennial herb belonging to the mint family (see facing page). The most common species is *Perilla frutescens*, which is mainly grown in India, China, Burma, Japan, and, more recently, in California. The leaves can be green or purple depending on the variety, and resemble slightly rounded stinging nettle leaves, with serrated edges. The plant is increasingly called by its Japanese name, *shiso*. In China it is called *su-tzu*.

Perilla oil is obtained from the seeds. The seeds do not all ripen at the same time, and those that ripen early tend to shed. When the majority of the fruits are mature the plants are cut and either bundled or spread on the ground to dry. After drying they are threshed. The seeds are roasted and crushed using a stone roller and the shell is manually winnowed off. The seeds contain between 35 and 50 percent oil. The residue seed cake is used as animal feed.

Perilla oil is used along with synthetic resins in the production of varnishes; it dries quickly and forms a hard, yellowish coating. It is also important in the manufacture of printing inks and linoleum.

Perilla oil is a very rich source of linolenic acid (between 50 and 70 percent) and this has now attracted a wider interest in the oil as a possible health supplement.

AT-A-GLANCE INFO

NUTRITIONAL HIGHLIGHT: Good source of linoleic acid (Om-6)

COUNTRY OF ORIGIN: China and Japan

STORAGE: Poor storage properties

ALTERNATIVE: Flax seed oil or hemp oil

RECOMMENDED: Currently local use only, but could be developed as a health oil.

PEQUI OIL

Pequi oil is a seed oil extracted from the seeds of the *Caryocar brasiliense*, which is a tree native to Brazil of the same species as the pecan nut tree (see page 37). It needs a tropical climate and grows in the Amazonian basin and surrounding areas. The tree yields a fruit about the size of an orange, with a fibrous husk. Inside, there are between 1 and 4 kidney-shaped brown kernels, which look like Brazil nuts. The kernels are coated with a pale yellow fat known locally as *suari* and the oil from the kernel itself is also highly prized by the local population.

Although the husk can be removed easily, the shell of the kernel is extremely difficult to crack. As soon as the fruit is harvested the suari fat is quickly extracted and used directly as a cooking oil to halt the activation of enzymes, which would make the fat turn rancid. The kernels are eaten or used by the indigenous population to extract the oil by means of cold pressing without solvent extraction. The remaining fruit is made into a liquor and the shell is used for fuel. The oils are also used in scalp preparations.

Both the suari and the pequi kernel oil are rich in oleic and palmitic fatty acids with linolenic and stearic acids in much smaller amounts. In Brazil, there are projects among indigenous groups to develop pequi oil production as a means of economic development.

AT-A-GLANCE INFO

NUTRITIONAL HIGHLIGHT: Good source of oleic acid (Om-9); also palmitic acid (saturated)

COUNTRY OF ORIGIN: Brazil

STORAGE: Store out of direct light

ALTERNATIVE: Brazil nut oil

RECOMMENDED: Currently local use only, but could be developed for wider use.

SUNFLOWER OIL

The plant, *Helianthus annuus*, is a member of the daisy family and is native to North America. It is grown primarily for its oil-rich seeds that are eaten roasted as a snack food or pressed to make an oil. Its beautiful, large yellow flower head is synonymous with regions of southern Europe where these fields of gold seemingly stretch for miles. Whilst the plant is associated with a sunny climate, there are variants which survive a range of temperatures. Today the biggest producers of the sunflower are Argentina, the US, and Europe.

The sunflower is well-known and much loved for its height (up to 11½ feet) and the size of its flower head (up to 29½ inches in diameter). The heads follow the sun throughout the day, turning to face its rays—the French name *tournesol* implies this behavior. The brown-black center of the flower contains hundreds of oil-rich seeds.

A range of sunflower varieties exist with differing fatty acid compositions, and so several types of sunflower oils are available:

Linoleic sunflower oil, which typically has at least 65 percent polyunsaturated fatty

AT-A-GLANCE INFO

NUTRITIONAL HIGHLIGHT: Variable—see text; vitamin E

STORAGE: Store in a cool dark place, for 12 to 18 months, but check use by date on label.

ALTERNATIVE: Grapeseed oil

RECOMMENDED: Try Flora Pure Sunflower Oil, or Mazola Organic Pure Sunflower Oil for a clean, fresh flavor and pale gold color, or La Tourangelle Organic Sunflower Oil.

A field of sunflowers

acids, containing, primarily, linoleic acid. This is the original sunflower oil and until recently has been the most common type of sunflower oil available. It has low saturated fat levels (about 13 percent), a clean, light taste, and is high in vitamin E. It is clear and pale golden in color. Domestically, it is an excellent choice for any liquid oil application such as dressings, shallow- and stir-frying, and baking. Commercially, it is used to make margarine and vegetable shortening but due to the high levels of polyunsaturated fats in linoleic sunflower oil, the oil is susceptible to oxidation during commercial usage, especially frying. Like other highly polyunsaturated oils, such as soybean (see page 88) and canola (see page 46), it can be hydrogenated into a more stable form.

High oleic sunflower oil is very high in monounsaturates. It is usually defined as having a minimum 80 percent oleic acid. The oil is clear, lightly golden, and has a neutral flavor. It is very stable without hydrogenation. It has many uses including bakery applications, spray-coating oils for cereal, crackers, and dried fruit, and is used in non-dairy creamers and many types of frying.

NuSun® sunflower oil is a relatively new oil on the block. It is stable without partial hydrogenation and has been developed for commercial use as a healthy alternative that performs like, and has all the characteristics of, an oil for home kitchen use. NuSun® oil is lower in saturated fat (less than 10 percent) than linoleic sunflower oil and has higher oleic levels (55 to 75 percent), with the remainder being linoleic acid. It is classified as a mid-oleic oil.

The cake remaining after the sunflower seeds have been processed for oil is used as a livestock feed. Sunflower oil is also used as a carrier oil for aromatherapy oils and in the cosmetic industry, particularly in skincare.

NIGER OIL

Obtained from a plant of the same family as the sunflower, *Guizotia abyssinica*, niger is of East African origin and grows from Ethiopia to Malawi. It has been extensively introduced to India and also to Pakistan and Bangladesh. It grows well in poor soil with very little rainfall.

It is a short, upright annual herb, about 3 feet high, with yellow Michaelmas daisy-like flowers. Each flower head produces 15 to 30 oil-bearing black, glossy seeds. The oil content of the seed varies greatly between 25 and 60 percent, depending on the variety.

The crop is cut using a sickle and then dried in the sun for 2 to 3 days. The seeds are removed by threshing, sometimes simply by hand which does little damage to the seed, but is obviously time consuming. In Ethiopia, oxen are sometimes used to tread out the seeds or to pull small threshing sledges.

Niger oil is pale yellow, odorless, and has a pleasant nutty taste. It contains several essential fatty acids but only linoleic acid in any great quantity. This gives it a short shelf life and it oxidizes quite quickly. In India, the oil is often used as an extender for sesame oil and sometimes as a substitute for ghee. It is also used in soap manufacturing.

AT-A-GLANCE INFO

NUTRITIONAL HIGHLIGHT: Good source of linoleic acid (Om-6)

COUNTRY OF ORIGIN: India and Ethiopia

STORAGE: Poor storage qualities; used fresh locally

ALTERNATIVE: Argan oil or sesame seed oil

RECOMMENDED: Not widely available—currently used locally only.

BUFFALO GOURD OIL

Buffalo gourd oil is extracted from the seeds of the *Cucurbita foetidissima*, which is native to south-west North America. As the Latin name of the plant indicates, this vine-like plant has a foul smell. It belongs to a species of wild gourds, which grow particularly well in the arid, desert conditions of Mexico and parts of the US.

The buffalo gourd produces yellow, hard-shelled fruit of up to about 3½ inches in diameter, which contain a white pulp and flat seeds ½ inch long. The plant has large starchy roots, which contain bitter glycosides, but these can be removed and the root used in starch production.

Traditionally, the seeds of the gourd were used by North American Indians to make soap and medicines. In cooking, the seeds can be ground into a powder and used as a thickening agent in soups or mixed with cereal flours when making cakes and cookies.

The seeds contain approximately 34 percent oil. The oil extracted is bland in odor and taste and varies from dark reddish brown to light yellow-green in color. After refining, it becomes a yellowish oil with a pleasant nutty taste.

The oil of buffalo gourd seed is becoming increasingly recognized as a potential commercial crop.

AT-A-GLANCE INFO

NUTRITIONAL HIGHLIGHT: Good source of oleic (Om-9) and linoleic acid (Om-6)

COUNTRY OF ORIGIN: North America

STORAGE: Good storage capabilites

ALTERNATIVE: Sunflower oil

RECOMMENDED: Currently only used commercially, but could be developed for wider use.

CHINESE TALLOW OIL

The deciduous Chinese tallow tree, *Sapium sebiferum*, grows in subtropical China and north India. The tree produces a fruit, which has 3 lobes. When it is ripe, it splits open to reveal a kernel about the size of a pea, surrounded by a solid fibrous, fatty pulp. The fruit offers 2 kinds of fat: the pulp yields a solid fat known as Chinese vegetable tallow, while the kernels contain a non-edible drying oil known as stillingia oil or *ting-yu* in China. Its structure allows the separation of the 2 oils with little contamination between them. Both the pulp and kernel are very high in fat—between 55–78 percent and 53–64 percent, respectively.

The fruits are hand picked and are left to dry in the sun until they blacken and split open. The seeds are removed by hand or with small threshers. In China, the seeds are steamed in perforated cylinders, which allows the melted fat to run off, after which they are crushed separately for the recovery of stillingia oil. Alternatively, the seeds are crushed between a fluted roller to strip off the outer seed coat without breaking the kernel.

In China, tallow oil is an edible oil known as *pi-yu*, which is rich in palmitic acid and a good supply of oleic acid. It is also used to make soap and candles.

ILLIPE (NUT) OIL (BUTTER)

The name originates from the Tamil language, and is a general term used to describe the oily nuts of a diverse collection of east Indian and South-east Asian trees. The 2 most important for their edible oils are the *Maduca longifolia* which grows in south India and Sri Lanka, and *M. indica*, which is a north Indian tree, well known in Bengal as the "Indian butter tree."

The trees flower in spring, and the long sweet tubular blossoms attract peacocks and other wildlife—the flowers can be harvested for making wine or as a dry food. Once the trees reach the age of about 8 years, they will begin to bear greenish fleshy fruit about the size of an egg and will continue to do so for about 60 years. The fruits contain between 1 and 4 seeds or nuts.

The oil from the nut resembles cocoa butter and is liquid in tropical climates but solidifies like coconut oil in cooler temperatures. It contains a good supply of oleic acid and useful amounts of palmitic and stearic acids. Illipe butter is also used for cooking in Malaysia and Indonesia, where product names ending with *kawang* contain the butter. Top grade illipe butter is exported on a small scale, and is usually sold under the name of "mowra butter" which is usually used in manufacturing margarine.

AT-A-GLANCE INFO

NUTRITIONAL HIGHLIGHT: Good source of oleic (Om-9); also palmitic acid (saturated)

COUNTRY OF ORIGIN: China

STORAGE: Store in a cool, dry place

ALTERNATIVE: Any vegetable oil

RECOMMENDED: In China, tallow oil is an edible oil known as *pi-yo*—available from specialist Oriental suppliers.

AT-A-GLANCE INFO

NUTRITIONAL HIGHLIGHT: Good source of oleic (Om-9); also palmitic and stearic saturated fatty acids

COUNTRY OF ORIGIN: Malaysia and Indonesia

STORAGE: Store in a cool, dry place

ALTERNATIVE: Palm oil

RECOMMENDED: Exported as "mowra butter"— available from specialist Asian suppliers.

MUSTARD SEED OIL

Mustard seed oil can be produced by pressing the seeds of black mustard, *Brassica nigra*, brown Indian mustard, *Brassica juncea*, and white mustard, *Brassica hirta*. It is an important cooking oil in India, Kashmir, and Bangladesh.

Mustard seeds contain about 30 percent oil, which is composed mostly of the fatty acids oleic acid, linoleic acid, and erucic acid. It is the second richest source of omega-3 fats after flax seed (linseed) oil (see page 41). The oil is brownish gold in color with a strong cabbage smell, and a hot nutty taste. Due to the erucic acid, which is considered noxious, mustard oil is not considered suitable for human consumption in the US, Canada, and the European Union. To get around the restriction in Western countries, the oil is often sold "for external use only" and "not for human consumption." A variety of mustard seed oil has been developed with a low content of erucic acid.

In India, mustard seed oil is generally heated almost to smoking before it is used for cooking, which reduces the strong smell and taste, and gives a smooth, mustard flavor which does not overpower other ingredients. It is used in curries, pickles, and sauces. In northern Italy, it is used in the fruit condiment called *mostarda*.

In northern India, mustard seed oil is also used for rubdowns and massages and is thought to improve blood circulation, muscular development, and be beneficial for the skin; the oil is also anti-bacterial.

AT-A-GLANCE INFO

NUTRITIONAL HIGHLIGHT: Lowest saturated fat of all oils; second richest source of linolenic acid (Om-3)

ALTERNATIVE: Sunflower oil with crushed toasted mustard seeds for flavor or for health reasons, flax seed or hemp oils

RECOMMENDED: Yandilla Mustard Seed Oil

SAFFLOWER OIL

Comes from the seed of a type of thistle, *Carthamus tinctorius*, related to the sunflower family. The thistle comes from west Asia. It looks like a thistle with deep orange, tufty flowers, which have been used as a clothes dye since the time of the ancient Egyptians. These tufts are also dried and used as a cheap saffron replacement known as "bastard saffron" which has the color but little of the flavor of the real spice (which is the dried stamens of a species of crocus flower). Safflower is cultivated in North Africa, China, India, and the US.

In the mid-18th century, the oil from the seeds began to attract attention due to its health benefits. Safflower seeds contain about 30 percent oil, and can be roasted and eaten as they are, but their oil after extraction is one of the richest sources of polyunsaturated fatty acids of any commonly available vegetable oil.

Safflower oil is a neutral oil with a light taste. It is very pale golden in color and makes an excellent light, all-round cooking oil with a long shelf life. Cold-pressed safflower oil is much more golden in color with a faint seedy aroma and light toasted-seed taste.

Safflower oil makes a good carrier oil in aromatherapy and has been used for the treatment of psoriasis and chapped or hardened skin.

AT-A-GLANCE INFO

NUTRITIONAL HIGHLIGHT: Good source of linoleic acid (Om-6)

COUNTRY OF ORIGIN: Various

STORAGE: Has a shelf life of about 2 years

ALTERNATIVE: Sunflower oil or extra virgin rapeseed oil

RECOMMENDED: Hain Safflower Oil or Clearspring Organic Unrefined Safflower Oil which is cold-pressed

PLUM SEED (KERNEL) OIL

This golden oil is relatively new on the general food market scene, but it has been used in the commercial confectionery industry in France as a replacement for almond essence for some time. It has a rich, sweet almond aroma and an amazingly marzipan-like flavor. It is 70 percent monounsaturated (oleic acid) and 23 percent polyunsaturated (linoleic acid). It is also rich in vitamin E. It is stable with a long shelf life, and can also be heated to 356°F.

This oil is an obvious choice for fresh fruit salads, chocolate desserts, custards, ice creams, and bakery items where an almond flavor is required. It goes particularly well with fresh plums, apricots, peaches, and strawberries. Try experimenting by mixing it with olive oil (see page 58) and verjuice (see page 115) for a vinaigrette to serve with fresh herbs and salad leaves scattered with toasted almonds. This oil is also delicious served with grilled fish and shellfish.

Plum seed oil is also used in the cosmetic industry. Its perfume and easy absorption make it a perfect choice for skin moisturizers and lip balms.

AT-A-GLANCE INFO

NUTRITIONAL HIGHLIGHT: Good source of oleic (Om-9) and linoleic acid (Om-6)

COUNTRY OF ORIGIN: France

STORAGE: As with all nut and seed oils, store out of the light in a cool, dark place and use by the manufacturer's recommended date.

ALTERNATIVE: For flavor, sunflower oil with a few drops of almond essence

RECOMMENDED: Try Perles de Gascogne Virgin Plum Seed Oil.

CAMELINA SEED OIL

The plant, *Camelina sativa* belongs to the family of the "Brassicaceae," and is recorded in cultivation documentation going back hundreds of years. Its Latin name means "cultivated," although its origins are as a wild weed found in Asia and Eastern Europe. Today it can be found growing in flax crops as a weed, and is commonly referred to as "weedseed."

Camelina seed oil (also known as "gold of pleasure") is rich in the essential fatty acids linoleic and oleic acids, and is low in saturated fat. It is cold pressed from the seeds of the annual plant, *Camelina sativa*. It has excellent moisturizing and replenishing properties and is therefore widely used in the cosmetic industry for skin products.

As a culinary oil, it is a pale, clear oil with a light fragrant aroma and flavor. Its excellent nutritional properties make it perfect for use in salad dressings and for cooking.

AT-A-GLANCE INFO

NUTRITIONAL HIGHLIGHT: Good source of linoleic acid (Om-6)

COUNTRY OF ORIGIN: Various

STORAGE: Store in a cool dark place, for 12 to 18 months, but check manufacturer's use by date.

ALTERNATIVE: Sunflower oil

RECOMMENDED: Not widely available—specialist oil manufacturers only.

AÇAI OIL

Açai is a native palm, *Euterpe oleracea*, of the Brazilian Amazonian region. Located in seasonally flooded areas and along water margins, the berry fruit of the tree are highly valued by the local Amazonian people as a juicing fruit, and have been considered an important part of their diet for centuries because of their unrivaled healing and nutritional properties. Once açai berries were launched into the wider world, this exotic sounding berry soon gained a reputation as a "super" food. It certainly boasts an impressive nutritional content, containing several vitamins including vitamins C and E along with potassium, copper and zinc.

Açai oil is coldpressed from the pulp of the berry. The pulp is deep red to purple in color with a hint of oil on the surface.

The oil is most comparable to grapeseed oil (see page 33); it is dark greenish brown in color with a mild fruity aroma and flavor. It can be used at low to medium cooking temperatures—rather like extra virgin olive oil. At the moment, the oil is most widely used in the cosmetic industry, but it won't be long before it hits the shelves as a new culinary sensation.

AT-A-GLANCE INFO

NUTRITIONAL HIGHLIGHT: Good source of linoleic acid (Om-6).

COUNTRY OF ORIGIN: Brazil

STORAGE: Store in a cool dark place, for 12 to 18 months, but check manufacturer's use by date.

ALTERNATIVE: Grapeseed oil or extra virgin olive oil

RECOMMENDED: Not widely available - currently only used commercially, but may soon be available for its health benefits.

WHEAT GERM OIL

The oil extracted from the germ of the wheat kernel, *Triticum aestival*, is very nutritional. Wheat germ oil is particularly high in octacosanol which behaves like a natural anabolic steroid by increasing oxygen utilization during exercise and increasing stamina, as well as improving reaction time. It also has a role to play in reducing blood cholesterol.

For the production of wheat germ oil, the wheat germs are carefully separated from the kernels during milling and are stabilized to avoid deterioration before extraction. Rarely, wheat germ oil is produced by cold pressing only, but it is a very perishable product and is not commercially available. Because of the huge grain processing facilities in the mid-west of the US, most wheat germ is produced there.

As an edible oil, wheat germ oil is quite strongly flavored, thick textured, and dark golden yellow in color. It is also expensive and easily perishable. It is usually taken as a health supplement, but can also be drizzled over salads and cooked meals prior to eating in order to boost nutrition. It is not an oil for cooking with.

For many years wheat germ oil has made a mark in the cosmetic industry; because of its richness in vitamin E, it is used in many skincare products and aromatherapy treatments.

AT-A-GLANCE INFO

NUTRITIONAL HIGHLIGHT: Rich source of vitamin E and octacosanol

COUNTRY OF ORIGIN: US

STORAGE: Follow manufacturer's guidelines

ALTERNATIVE: No direct alternative; nearest alternative is flax seed or hemp oils

RECOMMENDED: A. Vogel Wheat Germ Oil

VEGETABLE OIL

Vegetable oils are substances derived from plants and are liquid at room temperature. Although many different parts of plants may yield oil, in actual commercial practice oil is extracted primarily from the seeds of oilseed plants.

The generic term "vegetable oil" when used to label a cooking oil product refers to a blend of a variety of oils, and the most commonly used are soybean, rapeseed, sunflower, corn (maize), and palm kernel oils. Where they appear in pre-packed food, these oils will have been refined. Nutritional content, color, and flavor will be dependent on the oils used in the blend. It is advisable to check the label if you are concerned about the use of GM foods in your diet, as you may find that modified oilseeds are used in these blends. In general, "vegetable oil" is marketed as a general purpose cooking oil, suitable for frying, roasting, and baking. It will not enrich your food with flavor or color like some other oils, but offers a useful neutral medium for everyday cooking.

AT-A-GLANCE INFO

NUTRITIONAL HIGHLIGHT: Variable

COUNTRY OF ORIGIN: Various

STORAGE: Shelf life of about 2 years

ALTERNATIVE: Corn, rapeseed, or soybean oils

RECOMMENDED: Try Crisp 'n' Dry or Crisco Vegetable Oil.

SACHA INCHI OIL

BABASSU OIL

An Amazonian herbaceous vine, *Plukenetia Volubilis*, native to the high altitude rain forests of the Andean regions of South America. The plant is depicted on pottery found buried in Inca and pre-Inca tombs, dating back thousands of years.

Sacha inchi is a legume with branched nitrogen-fixing root nodules. It has white flowers, which develop into 4-sided green pods. The pods dry on the vine and contain 4 flat round seeds about the size of a penny. The seeds contain a substance that gives them a bitter taste if not roasted.

The oil extracted from the seeds is golden yellow in color and has been used by the Chanca Indians of Peru and also in parts of Africa for culinary use. It is also rubbed onto the skin to revitalize it and give a youthful appearance, and as a muscle soother for rheumatic pain. The oil cake is used for animal feed after oil extraction.

Nutritionally, sacha inchi oil contains a high quantity of omega-3, linolenic acid, and 35 percent linoleic acid (omega-6). This oil is currently being considered for greater commercial availability as a health supplement.

The babassu tree, *Orbignya oleifera*, is a tall palm tree native to the south-east region of the Amazon jungle in Brazil (see facing page). The tree is locally known as the "tree of life" as it is a source of fuel, food, animal feed, and building materials. The palms grow in natural forests, which are important to the environmental eco-balance of the area.

The babassu palm produces fruit in large bunches containing, on average, 200 individual fruits and each tree produces 1 to 5 bunches each year. Production starts at around 8 years old.

The kernel yields 60 to 70 percent of an oil, which is somewhat similar to coconut oil. It is virtually colorless and clear, and is fixed and stable. It becomes a soft solid, like petroleum jelly, below 75.2°F, and becomes white in color. It also has a fatty, nutty odor.

The refined oil is used much like coconut oil, and is used in margarine production and for general food purposes. The crude oil is suitable for soap production and detergents, and is used for burning in lamps. High in lauric and myristic acids, it penetrates the skin readily and is widely used in the cosmetic industry.

AT-A-GLANCE INFO

NUTRITIONAL HIGHLIGHT: Good source of linolenic (Om-3) and linoleic acid (Om-6)

COUNTRY OF ORIGIN: Andean regions of South America, West Africa

STORAGE: Poor storage properties

ALTERNATIVE: Flax seed oil or hemp oil

RECOMMENDED: This oil is currently being considered for greater commercial availability as a health supplement.

AT-A-GLANCE INFO

NUTRITIONAL HIGHLIGHT: High saturated fat content

COUNTRY OF ORIGIN: Brazil

STORAGE: A stable oil, lasting up to 2 years in its solid form

ALTERNATIVE: Coconut oil

RECOMMENDED: Local use only in cooking; used in the cosmetic industry and for making margarine.

SOYBEAN OR SOYA (BEAN) OIL

The soybean (or soya bean in UK), *Glycine maximus*, is a species of legume native to east Asia. The name of the soybean comes from *sou*, meaning "big bean," and it is one of the 5 holy plants of the Chinese people. Today, it is globally one of the most important staple foods, particularly in China, Japan, and South-east Asia; alongside wheat and rice, it competes both nutritionally and commercially. It is the main source of cooking oil in the world.

Soybeans can be broadly classified as "vegetable" (garden) or "field" (oil) types. Vegetable types cook more easily, have a mild nutty flavor, better texture, are larger in size, higher in protein, and are lower in oil than field types. These varieties are usually made into tofu and other soy products. Unlike other

AT-A-GLANCE INFO

NUTRITIONAL HIGHLIGHT: Good source of linoleic (Om-6) and oleic acid (Om-9). An excellent source of vitamin E.

COUNTRY OF ORIGIN: Various

STORAGE: Store in a cool dark place, for about 2 years, but check use by date on label. For cold-pressed oil, always follow the manufacturer's guidance for storage and usage.

ALTERNATIVE: For the cold pressed variety choose a good quality rapeseed oil or other vegetable based oil.

RECOMMENDED: Try cold-pressed Clearspring Organic Soya Oil

beans, the soybean is classed as an oilseed; it has a protein content of about 35 percent, as well as an oil content of 20 percent, and contains little carbohydrate.

The soybean is an annual plant that varies in growth, habit, and height depending on variety. It may grow prostrate, not growing higher than 8 inches, or upright, up to 6½ feet in height. The pods, stems, and leaves are covered with fine brownish-gray hairs. The leaves are divided into 3, like clover leaves. The plant has small, self-fertile flowers of white, pink, or purple. The fruit forms as a hairy short pod that grows in small clusters and usually contains between 2 and 4 beans or "seeds." The seeds have a dark-colored seed coat and can vary in color inside from green, red, and brown to black, but the most common for oil production are colored pale golden yellow.

The beans selected for oil manufacture are of a high quality, and must be sound, clean, and de-hulled. There are 2 types of soybean oil. The purest is obtained by cold pressing. This gives a golden oil with a good depth of beany flavor and fresh aroma. It is not suitable for cooking, so should be used as a flavor enhancer for salads and cooked vegetables (especially spinach) or to enrich cooked bean, pulse, and grain dishes.

The most familiar soybean oil is a highly-refined product. The soybeans are cracked, adjusted for moisture content, rolled into flakes, and solvent-extracted with commercial hexane. The oil is then refined, blended for different applications, and sometimes hydrogenated. Soybean oils, both liquid and partially hydrogenated, are exported all round the world, often sold as "vegetable oil," or ending up in a wide variety of processed foods. The remaining soybean husks are used as animal feed. This refined soybean oil is lightly golden yellow and clear. It smells slightly sweet and tastes mildly of seeds. It is this blandness of flavor that makes it popular in food manufacturing and cooking. It

can be heated to a high temperature, so is more versatile than the cold-pressed variety and is interchangeable with other general cooking oils for roasting, baking, and deep-frying.

The soybean plant has courted its fair share of controversy in recent years. Research and production of genetically engineered soybeans, which can resist certain herbicides, have been developed and planted in parts of the US. Due to the relatively high content of linolenic acid, soybean oil oxidizes and spoils quite quickly, so is not ideal for everyday cooking situations. In the early 1990s, Iowa State University developed soybean oil with 1 percent linolenic acid in the oil, and by the early 21st century the first plants were grown commercially. If you have concerns over GM foods, always check the label for guidance as to the source. If the manufacturer uses GM free soybeans, they will most likely say so.

Nutritionally speaking, soybean oil is an excellent source of vitamin E. It contains about 60 percent polyunsaturated, 25 percent monounsaturated, and about 14 percent saturated fat.

Soybean oil is also used commercially in the manufacture of a wide range of products including glycerine, paints, soaps, rubber substitutes, plastics, printing ink, and insect repellent.

PALM OIL *AND* PALM KERNEL OIL

The palm tree, *Elaeis guineensis,* is the most important of the oil palms and the most productive of all plants supplying edible oil because it yields two types of oil. It grows in several hot, equatorial regions of the world, from places like Malaysia and Columbia to West Africa. Before the mid-19th century, palm oil was only important to parts of West Africa as a cooking oil; once its value as a lubricant and base for soap were recognized, it became desirable to the outside world. In recent years, palm oil has been rated as the second most widely produced edible oil, after soybean oil (see page 88); if demand continues, it is likely to become the most widely produced vegetable oil in the world.

Palm oil production is a basic source of income for many of the world's poor in rural areas of South-east Asia, Central and West Africa, and Central America. An estimated 1.5 million small farmers grow the crop in Indonesia, and about half a million people are directly employed in the palm oil business in Malaysia. Not only does the palm represent a pillar of these nation's economies but it is a catalyst for rural development and political stability. The rising demand is resulting in

AT-A-GLANCE INFO

NUTRITIONAL HIGHLIGHT: High in saturated fatty acids, also vitamins E and K and magnesium.

COUNTRY OF ORIGIN: Various

STORAGE: Store in a cool, dark place.

ALTERNATIVE: Coconut oil

RECOMMENDED: Refined palm oil has many commercial uses. Try Jungle Products Red Palm Oil and Wildcrafted Red Palm Oil or Carotino brand blend of red palm oil and Canola oil.

tropical forests being cleared to establish new palm plantations. Along with the illegal hunting trade, logging, and forest fires, including those associated with the rapid spread of palm oil plantations, the outlook could be very bleak for these unique, bio-diversely important, habitats. Environmental protection groups have accused the growth of new palm oil plantations of being responsible for peat forest destruction in Indonesia and for accelerating global warming. These habitats provide protection for endangered species and minority tribes, whose livelihoods depend on the existence of the forests. Many of the world's major food manufacturers have been cited as driving the demand for new palm oil supplies, partly for products that contain non-hydrogenated solid vegetable fats. Because of health concerns, consumers now demand fewer hydrogenated oils in food products that were previously high in trans-fat content.

In Africa, the situation is very different to Indonesia or Malaysia. It is claimed that the production of palm oil in West Africa is largely sustainable, mainly because it is undertaken on smallholder level. The United Nations Food and Agriculture program is encouraging small farmers across Africa to grow palm oil, because the crop offers opportunities to improve livelihoods and provide income. It has been suggested that a more proactive and productive strategy than the current confrontational approach is a better course of action for those with environmental issues; this involves investment of funds to help the very people that are threatened by the loss of their livelihoods if the palm industry declines.

The palm tree can grow up to 328 feet tall and live for 150 years. The tree produces a small nut-like fruit known as *dende*, which yields the palm's 2 types of oil. The *dende* grow in bunches like dates, and vary in color from gold and orange to black depending on the variety. The

Carotino Red Palm and Canola Oil

flesh within consists of an unpalatable fibrous oily pulp from which 1 type of oil is made, and the other oil comes from the black-shelled nut in the center, which contains a pale, oil-rich kernel.

Palm oil is an important component of margarine because it can be added to other fats to make them harden naturally, rather than the fats having to be altered chemically and thus becoming controversial trans-fatty acids. It is also an important component of many soaps, washing powders, and personal care products. In cooking, palm oil can be used for high heat sautéing, frying, and baking. It gives a good earthy flavor to curry dishes, rich spicy stews, and even tropical desserts.

Recently a new palm oil product has emerged. It is labeled as red palm oil and unlike crude palm oil it is refined using low temperature and high vacuum techniques, which retain all the nutrients of the palm fruit oil without the unpurified substances.

BALANITES OIL

Balanites or the desert date, *Balanites aegyptiaca*, has been used in Egypt for more than 4,000 years as a source of oil and medicine.

In order to survive the harsh desert conditions, the tree has deep roots. It lives for more than 100 years, and produces fruit annually for 3/4 of its life. The ripe fruit resembles a date in size and appearance.

The balanites tree is used locally for many products: the wood is used for making tools, furniture, and boats; the fruit pulp for sweets and beverages; the leaves as herbs; and the kernels are pressed to make a nutritional oil for cooking and medicines. The stem of the tree contains substances that are used locally as insecticides and pesticides.

Balanite oil is thick, golden yellow in color with a distinct aroma. It is fixed and stable. It contains a high percentage of linoleic acid and has a good oleic acid content. Despite its nutritional and medicinal value and other uses, balanite oil is practically unknown outside the growing regions.

There is great potential for the future because the oil contains a group of chemicals called saponins, which help control cholesterol in the blood as well as having anti-inflammatory and immune-stimulating activity. Beyond that, saponins demonstrate anti-microbial properties, particularly against fungi as well as bacteria and protozoa.

AT-A-GLANCE INFO

NUTRITIONAL HIGHLIGHT: Good source of linoleic acid (Om-6)

COUNTRY OF ORIGIN: East and West Africa; Sudan

ALTERNATIVE: Coconut oil

RECOMMENDED: Currently local use only

COHUNE PALM OIL

The cohune palm, *Orbignya cohune*, grows in the tropical climate of parts of South America where there is a high rainfall. The palms produce egg-shaped fruit in bunches. The fruit has an outer husk and a pulpy fibrous layer surrounding a nut. Inside the very hard nut shell is a kernel approximately 1 1/4 inches long, which contains about 70 percent oil. It is rich in lauric acid, and offers good supplies of myristic and oleic acids.

Most nuts are cracked by hand, an extremely laborious task as they are very hard, but machines have been developed to crack them. The oil is extracted by small expellers once the nuts are toasted, and is then refined.

Cohune palm oil is similar to coconut oil and is used locally in margarine production, baking, and cookie making. Damaged kernels are used as cattle feed, the shells as fuel, and press cake after oil extraction is also fed to animals.

AT-A-GLANCE INFO

NUTRITIONAL HIGHLIGHT: High in saturated fat and Oleic acid (Om-9)

COUNTRY OF ORIGIN: South America

ALTERNATIVE: Coconut oil

RECOMMENDED: Currently local use only

CORN OIL

Corn is the general name for cereal crops, and is commonly used in the US and elsewhere as the name for maize.

Corn oil has a milder taste and is less expensive than most other types of vegetable oils. It is clear and richly golden in color. It is a highly stable oil and retains its fresh flavor when properly stored at room temperature, and even when used in cooking at high temperatures—its high smoke point makes it a valuable and popular frying oil.

Corn oil is extremely versatile and can be used interchangeably with other vegetable oils. It has a light taste, which complements other flavors and can be used for salad dressings and marinades, baking, sautéing, stir-frying, and deep- or shallow-frying.

Commercially, corn oil is a key ingredient in some manufacturing. It is also one source of bio-diesel. This is more commonly made from soybean (see page 88) or rapeseed oil (see page 44), but as corn oil refining technology improves, it is expected to become a greater source in its own right as well as being a good backup source in case of large-scale soybean crop failures. Other industrial uses for corn oil include soap, salve, paint, rust-proofing for metal surfaces, inks, textiles, and insecticides. It is also sometimes used as a carrier for drug molecules in pharmaceutical preparations.

AT-A-GLANCE INFO

NUTRITIONAL HIGHLIGHT: Good source of oleic (Om-9) and linoleic acid (Om-6) and vitamin E.

COUNTRY OF ORIGIN: Various

STORAGE: Shelf life of about 12 months

ALTERNATIVE: Sunflower, rapeseed, or soybean oils

RECOMMENDED: Mazola Corn Oil

INFUSED/FLAVORED OILS

Conimex Wok Oil

Rustichella D'Abruzzo Limonolio

There are many flavored oils on the market today, some being more worthy of purchase than others. It's a matter of personal taste, of course, but it is worth considering that they take up valuable storage space in kitchen cupboards, and that flavoring ingredients are always better when added fresh; this way you will be able to enjoy the flavor of your chosen oil and the ingredients it is combined with as freshly as possible. However, some flavored oils do make sense as a convenient 2-in-1 solution, especially when a costly or rare ingredient is involved e.g. truffle—the infused oil on this occasion may offer you all the flavoring you need at a fraction of the price.

When choosing a flavored oil, especially if you are looking for a natural product, always read the ingredients label, and check for any artificial additives like colors, flavorings, and preservatives, which are sometimes used in inferior products. Infusing oils with herbs and spices is very easy to do yourself (see page 149). This way you can choose your base oil and exact flavor requirements to suit dishes that you cook most often.

Olive oil (see page 58) is often used as a base oil for flavoring, but its own flavor will be masked by whatever ingredients are added to it—it doesn't really make sense to buy or use an oil of exceptional quality for infusing because you won't be able to enjoy the full flavor of the oil itself. In general, medium-priced olive oils are best used for infusion purposes, or a light olive and sunflower oil (see page 74) mix. Most commonly, neutral oils like sunflower are used wherever the flavor of the added ingredient is meant to dominate.

HERE ARE SOME USEFUL FLAVORED OILS YOU MIGHT LIKE TO TRY:

Chinese chili oil—probably the commonest and most well-used of flavored oils. Usually chili is added to groundnut oil, and it is often reddish orange in color with a fiery chili kick. Use drop by drop as a finishing oil to add a dash of spice to stir-fries, noodles, soups, and stews.

Lemon oil—this is usually made in Italy and consists of fruity Italian olive oil flavored with lemon. It is a very zesty, aromatic oil, delicious drizzled over chicken and fish, or when used to liven up a mayonnaise or salsa.

RECOMMENDED: Try Rustichella d'Abruzzo Limonolio, pale yellow-green in color with a mild, creamy lemon note.

Chipotle chili oil—the Mexican version of the Oriental favorite. It is usually olive oil based with smoked paprika added to it as well as the fiery chili spice. Orange-yellow in color, it is smoky and aromatic. Use sparingly to add life to plain cooked rice, polenta, or noodles, or add to a dressing or salsa for barbecued food.

RECOMMENDED: Try the Cool Chile Co. Chipotle Chile Oil for a delicious smoked chili flavor with added garlic.

Truffle oil—usually olive oil based but sometimes sunflower oil is used for a more neutral base. This is an expensive oil enriched with either black truffle or even more extravagantly, white truffle (this is at least twice the price of its darker relative). Sometimes an "aroma" or flavoring is used to provide the intense mushroom flavor and earthy wafting notes of this oil, so check the label to see whether the price justifies the contents. Best used as a finishing for dishes, it is an excellent oil for tossing into freshly cooked pasta, finishing off a risotto, or for seasoning any dish containing mushrooms.

RECOMMENDED: Try Gocce di Peccato al Tartufo Nero from Umbria in Italy for a medium-flavored olive oil and fungi flavor enriched with garlic.

Wok oil—a useful kitchen standby product by Conimex made up of a blend of groundnut, palm, and coconut oil and a "secret" blend of herbs and spices, which is designed for high heating. It is clear, deep yellow-orange in color, smells of fenugreek and curry leaves, and adds a delicious savory aroma and taste to stir fries, rice, noodles, and barbecued meats.

Cool Chile co.
Chipotle Chile Oil

Gocce Di Peccato al
Tartufo Nero

95

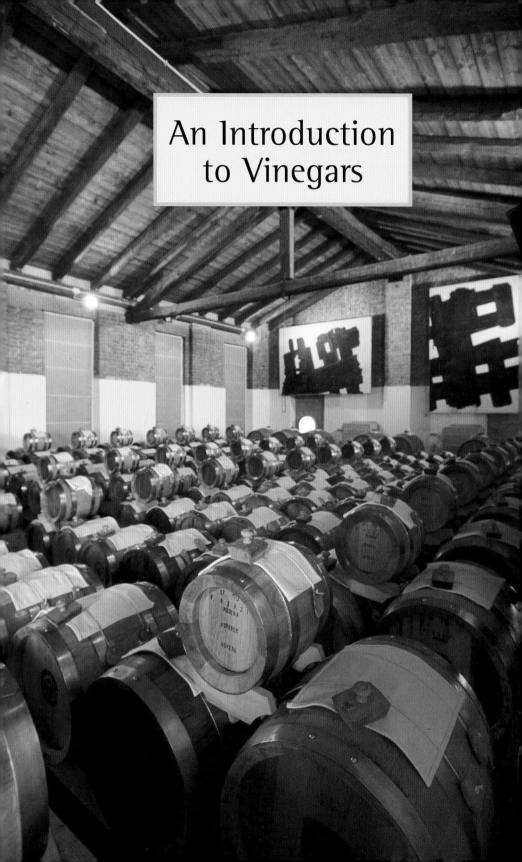

An Introduction
to Vinegars

VINEGAR—A BRIEF HISTORY

Vinegar used for pickling

The use of vinegar goes back a long way—it has been used throughout history, for thousands of years in fact. Its origins aren't completely certain, but it is more than likely that it was invented by accident. This is due to the fact that fruit and other plant juices turn sour naturally, and wine and vinegar were probably discovered at the same time. Ancient brewers looked to find a way to prevent their wine and other alcoholic beverages from souring—the word vinegar derives from the Latin *vinum* meaning wine and *acer* meaning sour: in French, *vinaigre*, literally means sour wine. They realized this was possible by restricting the wine's exposure to air. At the same time, our ancestors realized that the acidic liquid itself could have its uses and it was probably first used as a preservative. The Babylonians made vinegar from date and raisin wines, and they flavored it with herbs and spices to preserve meat and vegetables, and diluted it with water to take as a drink. The

Romans, too, drank a vinegar concoction with meals as a digestif, and as an antiseptic; they called it *posca*.

One of the earliest recordings of vinegar use is in the 5th century B.C., in the writings of Hippocrates, where he recommends it for medicinal use. The late Roman recipe book of Apicius contains references to using vinegar with honey as a seasoning and flavor enhancer. At the same time, in China, a different form of vinegar was developed from rice water and other grains like wheat and sorghum. *Chencu* or mature vinegar has been used as a flavoring and in medicine for over 1,000 years. In the Philippines, sour liquids from palm sap and tropical fruit juices were developed to serve with local raw fish, meats, and vegetables. Later, in the 15th century, in England and other beer-drinking parts of northern Europe, *ale-gar* was made. It was rich and dark, almost balsamic-like in texture, and similar to the robust Bavarian beer vinegars of today.

One of today's most respected and much loved vinegars, balsamic vinegar (see page 108), has a history dating back to the 11th century. The ancient art of making a sweet condiment from grape juice dates back to the Romans who invented the art of making *sapa*, a mixture made from boiled-down grape juice. However, it wasn't until the mid-11th century that reports appeared of a wood or balsamic vinegar from the region of Emilia Romagna, ruled by a family called Este. In these times, it was taken as a refined drink or as medicine, and was not made for commercial purposes. The wealthiest families of the region cared for their vinegars, perfecting them over the years, and passed them on as treasured heirlooms. They presented small vials to their friends and even bequeathed their vinegar to their daughters as a valuable part of their dowries. By the 18th century, the Este family had moved to Modena. It was then that the term *balsamico* began to be used for the regional specialty vinegar that had been aged in wooden barrels, to imbibe its aroma. By the turn of the next century, *balsamico* was considered a precious commodity. Surprisingly, it has only been in the last 30 years or so that the rest of the world has been able to sample this wonderful vinegar through its export from Italy.

For many years, vinegar was made very simply by allowing partly filled containers of wine, beer, and other alcoholic substances to sour naturally in the air. This would take from weeks to months but the result wasn't very dependable. By the 17th century, a method for aerating wine was invented and this was developed further over the coming years. The biggest breakthrough in vinegar history came in the 19th century, when French scientist Louis Pasteur was assigned the task of finding out how to keep wine and vinegar from deteriorating during production, storage, and transportation. He discovered the essential role of bacteria and oxygen in vinegar production, and his research brought about a revolutionary process for the commercial production of vinegar. Since then, vinegar production techniques have been developed further and current methods mean that some vinegar can be produced in a matter of hours and days rather than weeks.

Balsamic vinegar and olive oil

THE MANY USES OF VINEGAR

CHAMPION'S VINEGAR
IS THE BEST

Vinegar can be viewed as a panacea throughout history. It has certainly been used for a wide range of applications over the centuries, outside the kitchen. During the Middle Ages, it was used as a washing medium for treating many illnesses such as plague, fever, leprosy, and snake bite. In the late 19th century, vinegar was even used as (an unreliable) contraceptive by "ladies of the night." Many books on cleaning and laundry, including the famous *Mrs Beeton's Book of Household Management*, cite vinegar in many of its solutions from stain removal, fabric softening, cleaning an iron, deodorizing, cleaning windows and other surfaces, to modern day remedies for dissolving chewing gum, polishing chrome, freshening the air, and cleansing the hands of onion or garlic odors. A little drop of vinegar in a vase of water will help prolong the life of cut flowers; a drop on a cloth will help shine patent leather shoes; drinking a couple of spoonfuls a day in a little water may act as an insect repellent; and it will help to bring out the shine in your hair if used in the water during the final rinse when washing it.

Medicinally speaking, vinegar has been used for all sorts of complaints from acting as an antiseptic and an anti-fungal for sore throats, fungal infections, and head lice, to rubbing on joints to ease stiffness. Vinegar has be used as an aid to combating fatigue and as a cure for insomnia; it can ease stomach upsets and help sooth insect bites and sunburn. During World War I, vinegar was used to treat wounds on the battlefields and in the makeshift hospitals.

Back in the kitchen, there are many culinary applications and recipes that include vinegar, and with all the different flavors available now, the combination of tastes is vast. Apart from the obvious dressings, sauces, and marinades, vinegar can be used:

- in sweet and savory chutneys and pickles
- as a tenderizer in marinades and the cooking water for meat, such as boiled ham
- in salsas and sweet and sour sauces
- as a glaze with oil and honey for brushing

over meat and fish prior to broiling or barbecuing
- as a dipping agent to serve with olive oil, pickles, raw vegetable crudités, and fresh bread
- as an ingredient in traditional cake, cookies, and pie recipes
- as a flavor enhancer for sweet berries and other ripe fruit
- to enrich the flavor of lemon or lime in a custard or curd tart
- to add an extra flavor note to a berry or melon sorbet
- as an agent to prevent fruit and vegetable discoloring
- to fork through rice to make the grains separate and make the rice fluffier in texture
- as a refreshing drink, diluted with water and sweetened with honey—it is particularly good when added to homemade lemonade to help enhance the zestiness.

Today, vinegars are made from a wide range of products, all over the world. They vary in strength, flavor, and color depending on what base ingredient is used, and also how the vinegar is stored, or if it is matured. Rice vinegars are among the mildest flavored, whilst wine, cider, and beer varieties are much stronger. Some of the more unusual vinegars are made from sugar cane, syrups, honey, fruit, and vegetable juices, even flower sap. It is worth giving a bit more thought to your purchase next time you reach for your favorite condiment and perhaps think about exploring the world of vinegars in greater depth.

SIMPLE VINEGAR CHEMISTRY

The oxidation of ordinary alcohol (ethyl alcohol or ethanol) produces acetic acid, the essential constituent of vinegar. Acetic acid gives vinegar its acidic flavor and classic pungent aroma. It is essentially a preserving agent—just 1 teaspoon of standard vinegar mixed with 9 fl oz water will be strong enough to inhibit the growth of many standard household microbes. The particular color and flavor of the vinegar product also depends on the raw material used and on any substances added.

In a very basic sense, when wine or other alcoholic liquid is exposed to the air it turns sour; this is because bacteria in the air invade the liquid and are able to use alcohol as an energy source. Their metabolism causes the formation of acetic acid and water. Because the bacteria need air in order to survive, they live on the surface of the liquid, and along with other microbes, they help form a thick scum, which is known as "mother." Not all bacteria give a satisfactory vinegar, and modern-day production techniques ensure that a careful balance is maintained by adding vinegar from a previous batch to the liquid to be fermented. This "starter" contains the mother. Bacteria of the genus *Acetobacter* and *Gluconobacter* (mainly *A. pasteurianus* and *A. aceti*) are the most commonly used bacteria in vinegar production.

The strength of the alcoholic liquid used determines the acetic acid content of the final vinegar, and also the length of time the fermentation process takes—the higher the alcohol content the more the bacteria are inhibited. Alcoholic beverages stronger than 10 to 12 percent proof are usually diluted with water in order to keep production times to a minimum. A concentration of 5 percent alcohol will give a vinegar with about 4 percent acetic acid which is stable enough to keep well and strong enough to give good flavor.

VINEGAR PRODUCTION

Vinegar production

There are 3 basic methods used in the western world for making vinegar. The oldest is the "Orléans process." It is a simple method developed in Orléans, France, during the Middle Ages. At the time, barrels of wine were transported up the river to Paris. Due to the slow transit time, the heat, and poor quality of some of the wine, the contents had turned to vinegar by the time the barrels reached their final destination (see Vinaigre d'Orléans, page 116). The discovery of sour wine was harnessed into a production technique, and today some of the best vinegar is made in this way. Wooden barrels are partly filled with 3 parts good quality wine to 2 parts vinegar and inoculated with mother of vinegar, then left to ferment. The bacterial organisms slowly turn the wine to acetic acid without adding any heat; this helps preserve the flavor of the wine in the final vinegar. Periodically, some of the product is drawn off and is replaced with new wine. This slow process takes about 2 months to yield a barrel of vinegar. It is an expensive production method, but does give a fine superior product, which will sell for a justifiably high price.

The "trickling method" involves wine being slowly sprinkled repeatedly over a porous, aerated surface such as wood shavings or other similar synthetic material. The bacteria build up all over the surface, and become incorporated into the wine as it dribbles over. At the same time, the wine is exposed to plenty of oxygen in order to speed up the process. Quite a lot of heat is generated during this technique and this destroys any of the finer, more volatile flavors of the original wine. However, this method is quick and takes only a few days to turn wine into a reasonable-quality vinegar.

Finally, the quickest method of all, the "submerged culture method" can turn alcoholic liquid into acetic acid in 1 or 2 days. This is a heavy industrial process that involves passing bacteria directly into a tank of vinegar by means of a bubbling air process. The resulting product is inexpensive but lacks the flavor and aroma of other more slowly produced vinegars.

Once vinegar is made, just about every type for general consumption is pasteurized at 150°F. This destroys any remaining bacteria and helps preserve the qualities and stability of the final product.

VINEGAR STORAGE

The acetic acid content of vinegar means that it will store well without needing to be refrigerated. White wine vinegar keeps very well without any change in color or flavor. Other vinegars may develop sediment or become cloudy over time, but this will not affect the vinegar and it can still be used with confidence. As with most culinary ingredients, keep your vinegar well sealed and out of direct sunlight—ideally in a dark kitchen cupboard or at room temperature on a work surface away from any windows. Remember, if you decant vinegar into another vessel, the acid content makes it corrosive so avoid contact with metals or aluminum. Glass, sturdy plastic, wood, enamel, or stainless steel are the best materials for keeping vinegar. Always check manufacturer's storage instructions for any specific information—this is especially important for gourmet vinegars.

Vinegar decanted into glasses

WINE VINEGAR

Vinaigre de Reims Clovis

Vino vinaigre de Chardonnay

This vinegar is most prominent in areas of the world where red and white wine is produced in quantity, and just as there are different qualities of wine, there are also varying standards of vinegar products. The best varieties start with a good quality wine and follow the Orléans process (see page 101). Slow fermentation in oak casks for several years produces a rich depth of flavor, and if made in small batches, with due care and attention, they will have more subtle, complex aromas and a mellow edge—and a heftier price tag, of course.

Commercially produced wine vinegars are of an inferior quality. Cheaper wines are often used, and large-scale production techniques (see page 101) are faster but remove many of the complexities of flavor, giving a much harsher acidity to the finished vinegar.

Red wine vinegar, like the wine, is a stronger-tasting, more robustly flavored vinegar than white which has a moderately tangy flavor.

Single grape varieties are more expensive than blended wine products. Generally speaking, red and white vinegars can be used like most other

AT-A-GLANCE INFO

ACID CONTENT: 6-7 percent

ALTERNATIVE: For red wine vinegar use sherry vinegar or white wine vinegar; for white wine vinegar use cider vinegar; for champagne vinegar use 1 part white wine vinegar to 2 parts water.

STORAGE: Keep well sealed, out of direct sunlight, preferably in the cool. Should keep indefinitely but always check manufacturer's use by date.

RECOMMENDED: For Italian wine vinegars try the Olitalia brand and for Spanish try the brand by Unio. Martin Pouret leads the way in French wine vinegar production.

WINE VINEGAR

Wine vinegar

vinegars in dressings, sauces, and marinades, and as a base for flavoring with herbs, spices, and fruits etc. White wine vinegar is used to accompany lighter flavored ingredients and where the color of a dish is to be preserved; it is the vinegar of choice for the classic egg, butter, and tarragon based French sauce, Bearnaise.

When it comes to choosing a variety of wine vinegar, there are many types available, in fact, enough to make you think you were in a liquor store rather than a grocer's. Here are some of the ones you may come across:

Banyuls—a smooth, slightly sweet vinegar from the Banyuls region in southern France, which is famous for its dessert wines. This vinegar is made from white grenache, muscat, and gray grenache grapes. Aged in wooden barrels for 6 years, its production is limited, but the vinegar is well worth seeking out for its nutty flavor and deep golden color. It combines well with nut or

olive oils in a vinaigrette, and is a good deglazer after cooking game and red meats. Lovely over roasted or barbecued vegetables, or as a fish and lean poultry marinade.

Bordeaux—probably the most widely known and used of the red wine vinegars. It has a strong, powerful flavor and full-bodied red color. Excellent as a dressing for oily fish like sardines and mackerel or foods cooked on a charbroiler.

Cabernet Sauvignon—rich burgundy in color, the robust red wine gives a unique full-bodied flavored vinegar, ideal for use in meat marinades and dressings.

Champagne—a premium vinegar; expensive, with a delicate, refined flavor. Pale golden in color, clear, bright, and light with a mild flavor. Best used with subtle flavors like chicken, fish, or for dressing a light salad.

Chianti wine vinegar

Vino Moscatel wine vinegar

Chardonnay—a pale to medium honey-gold colored white vinegar with a slightly perfumed aroma depending on the oakiness and origin of the original wine. 6 percent acidity. Use like Champagne vinegar, but it is also good lightly sprinkled over ripe berry fruit and melon, and its fresh edge works well in stocks and sauces to serve with pork and oily fish.

Chianti—an Italian robustly fruity red wine vinegar. Good with blue cheese, mushrooms, beef steaks, and game meats, along with classic Italian recipes.

Lambrusco—made from the light sparkling wine typical of the Emilia-Romagna region of Italy. It is a light ruby color with a delicately floral flavor which makes it the right condiment for everyday gourmet dishes, especially salads.

Merlot—dark red color with a unique delicate flavor and aroma. Highly prized as being one of the best to use in the kitchen.

Moscatel—made from Moscatel wine and concentrated must of Moscatel grapes which gives a complex and aromatic vinegar with rich floral notes and hints of peaches and honey. Rich sherry-brown in color with 6 percent acidity. Goes well with anything—the perfect all rounder.

Pinot Noir—bright, medium red in color; one for the connoisseur as it is hard to beat, with a distinctly fruity flavor.

Prosecco—produced from the prestigious Italian Prosecco wine, bright golden in color with a dry, perfumed aroma and flavor. This gourmet vinegar is perfectly matched with salads and lightly-cooked vegetables, fish, and chicken.

Unio Vermouth wine vinegar

Martin Pouret aged red wine vinegar

Shiraz—a spicy and currant-flavored red wine vinegar from Australia aged in oak barrels to give a richer, more intense flavor.

Vermouth—deep sherry-brown color, 6 percent acidity, with a unique herby/spice aroma and delicate flavor. Use to dress a fresh herb salad, or drizzle over sweet fruit desserts to add an extra zing.

Vinaigre a l'Ancienne—this literally means "aged vinegar." Vinaigre de vin rouge vieille reserve by Martin Pouret (see Vinaigre d'Orleans page 116) is an aged red wine vinegar made with the traditional Orleans process. It has a superior, full aromatic flavor, with a higher 7 percent acidity content, compared to standard commercially produced, less complex blends.

Vinaigre de Reims—produced from wine of the region in France, and is an ingredient of the mustard of the same name. Both vinegar and mustard have been highly regarded since the 18th century. Golden honey colored with a fresh aroma, 7 percent acidity, and slightly woody flavor with a mild honey note. The Clovis brand is aged for a year in oak barrels, and has a natural sediment which makes the product look slightly cloudy. Ideal for salad dressings and serving with poultry, pasta, and shellfish.

Zinfandel—an artisan red wine vinegar made in California by the Orleans process and aged for 2 years in oak. This gives a reddish brown vinegar with a slightly spicy, fruity flavor. Recommended for use as a dressing for avocados and roast vegetables.

BALSAMIC VINEGAR

Gran Deposito aceto balsamico di Modena Giuseppe Giusti

The true vinegar is produced only in the provinces of Modena and Reggio-Emilia, in the Emilia-Romagna region of northern Italy. Balsamic means "like balsam"—balsam being an aromatic resin—and authentic balsamic vinegar is so named because it is thick (resin-like) and aromatic.

The highest standard of vinegar making in Italy is known as Aceto Balsamico Tradizionale (ABT) and this was introduced in 1986 (prior to this time, it was referred to as Aceto Balsmico Naturale). Its production is subject to a Denominazione di Origine Controllata (DOC—Protected Geographical Indication), which essentially restricts production to the 2 provinces of Modena and Reggio-Emilia. In 2000, exact criteria for making an ABT was established and a Denominazione di Origine Protetta (DOP—Protected Denomination of Origin) was created.

AT-A-GLANCE INFO

ACID CONTENT: About 8 percent

ALTERNATIVE: Black rice vinegar; sherry vinegar; red wine vinegar plus sugar or honey; Vincotto®; agridulce; fig vinegar

RECOMMENDED: For a good everyday balsamic vinegar try Acetaia Sereni Aceto Balsamico di Modena; Giuseppe Giusti Aceto Balsamico 6 year old, 8 year old, and 12 year old are a little bit more special and a small 1½ fl oz bottle of Acetaia San Giacomo's Riscopritti Balsamico, a *condimento*, is more special still—this is made from the must only and is an ideal size (and price) to introduce yourself to the world of aged balsamic.

BALSAMIC VINEGAR

Acetaia Sereni Balsamic vinegar of Modena

Unfortunately, the market has been flooded by poor-quality imitations bearing the balsamic name and these often have only the merest trace of the characteristics of the real thing. True ABT is made only from the "must" (or *mosto* in Italian), which is the pressed unfermented juice of, most usually, the Trebbiano grape. Sometimes other grapes may be used, these being Lambrusco, Ancellotta, Sauvignon, and Sgavetta. Trebbiano grapes have a high sugar content. The must is immediately boiled down in open pots over a direct flame at a minimum of 176°F (stipulated by the DOP) to insure that all the bacteria is killed—if the must is cooked at too high a temperature, then the sugar may caramelize and this will lead to an undesirable taste in the finished product. Different producers within the 2 regions vary the length of time the must is heated and the temperature to which is heated.

This makes a fruity syrup with a sugar content of between 28 and 33 percent. At this point the must is added to the "mother barrel" or *botte Madre*. This contains bacterial colonies from previous batches which, along with warmth from the sun, causes fermentation into vinegar. Nothing else is added.

According to DOP rules, it then has to be aged in barrels of different sizes and woods—first in 1, then transferred to another, and so on. The type of wood to be used is not specified, but most producers will vary the barrels for the different flavor and color characteristics the wood adds. The first barrel used is called the *Rincalzo* and it is filled to $^{3}/_{4}$ full or more. The second barrel phase is the *Traverso*, with the transfer from the first barrel taking place anytime after 12 months. As the vinegar matures, it decreases in volume due to evaporation, and is transferred to smaller and smaller barrels to compensate, each barrel's wood adding another layer of flavor to the finished vinegar. This cycle continues until the

French bread, oil and balsamic vinegar

smallest barrel is reached. After a minimum of 12 years (or beyond, even 75 to 100 years), the process of *Prelievo* can take place, when a small amount of the precious fluid is removed and sent to the Consorzio for judging. If the 5-panel board award sufficient points, the vinegar can be officially bottled, with a hefty surcharge to prevent any adulteration, and it is returned to the producer as a saleable ABT. The final product is a dark, thick vinegar or *condimento*, which has a mellow flavor, and while it still retains a good vinegar "bite," the harshness has been removed.

Some of the most commonly used woods for the barrels are: chestnut, which aids coloration and acidity development; cherry gives sweetness; juniper and mulberry provide a spicy aroma; and oak prevents too much evaporation. The DOP standards clearly

prohibit the addition of any aromas, flavors, colors, and chemicals, so the combination of wood is very important to give a good all-round balanced product.

It is worth noting at this point that balsamic vinegars without the ABT designation on the label are made commercially, sometimes with "di Modena" on the label. They are usually either stored for 6 months to a year in stainless steel tanks, or aged for 2 to 12 years in wooden barrels. There are no standards or controls other than those of the DOP, so unless you read the label you could be buying any combination of red wine vinegar, concentrated grape juice, sugar, water, preservatives, caramel, and flavorings to make something only very vaguely approximating the Tradizionale. If you do want to buy an ABT, here is a quick checklist:

1   Look out for "must" as the only ingredient on the label.
2   Check the age—at least 12 years.
3   Note the production location—Modena or Reggio-Emilia.
4   Look out for the ABT designation.
5   Finally, the higher the price, the more aged and traditional the vinegar.

If you can't afford one of the aged balsamics, buy the most aged/expensive balsamic you can justify to yourself. This is not to do with food snobbery, but with personal enjoyment. The aged balsamics are more concentrated and have strong flavors, so a little goes a long way; you will find that the younger ones are lighter and require a more generous splash to season.

There are reports of 11th-century Italian producers maturing their vinegar products for over 100 years, and there were times when balsamic vinegars were so highly prized that they were never sold; they could only be acquired as a dowry, as an assessment of a bride's worth. For many years, aged balsamics

Bouquet methode balsamique fig bouquet

have been taken as a digestif after a rich meal, by those who can afford them; this is a particular practice of the wealthy older ladies of the Modena region. Males of the region consider the vinegars an aid to virility. In both circumstances, the aged balsamics are taken by the glass.

Balsamic vinegar has a high acid level, but the sweetness disguises the tart flavor, and makes it very mellow. It is best regarded as a condiment or seasoning rather than a vinegar. For this reason, it makes an excellent low-fat salad dressing, especially for strongly flavored or bitter leaves like arugula, chicory, or endive. It is delicious sprinkled over ripe soft fruits such as strawberries, peaches, and sweet melon, and makes an unusual talking point spooned over good-quality vanilla ice cream. It can also be used as a flavoring in cooking, where small amounts can add a depth of both flavor and color—add toward the end of cooking and never boil it as this will taint the flavor. Vintage balsamics are best served with shavings of mature Parmesan cheese, or as a dressing for gravadlax, or beef or tuna carpaccio.

Flavored balsamic vinegars are now also available with additions such as garlic, chili, fig, and vanilla. All have their particular niche in the market and, as with flavored wine vinegars, the world is your oyster when it comes to the flavorings of the future.

WHITE BALSAMIC VINEGAR

There are two types of balsamic products that fall into this category: one that is often labeled simply as white balsamic, and one that is clearly called white balsamic vinegar. Although the two look very similar, the former is usually regarded as a condiment because it is a blend of sweetened white wine vinegar with grape juice and preservative.

White balsamic vinegar, like classic balsamic, is usually produced in Modena but is made from a different process than regular balsamic vinegar. The resulting vinegar is a clear, light straw color or pale golden and the flavor is sweet and fresh. Quality white balsamic vinegar may have a delicate perfumed aroma and taste.

Use in exactly the same way you would any other sweet vinegar where you want a hint of syrupy flavor. Ideal for finishing light meats and fish in the pan or for adding to sauces and dressings when you don't want to color the food with a traditional, dark balsamic vinegar—for example, as a seasoning for shellfish, cooked chicken, or mozzarella. The flavor also lends itself well to citrus and herb flowers such as lavender or rose—try blending floral flavors with white balsamic and honey as a dressing for fruit salads.

AT-A-GLANCE INFO

ACID CONTENT: 5 percent

ALTERNATIVE: White wine vinegar or sherry vinegar plus sugar or honey

STORAGE: Keep well sealed, out of direct sunlight, preferably in the cool, for up to 2 years or more but always check manufacturer's use by date.

RECOMMENDED: Belazu White Balsamic (this is a good quality condiment from Modena) or Roland Premium White Balsamic Vinegar from Modena, an authentic vinegar.

VINCOTTO®

An Italian word that means "cooked wine" which is now a registered trademark of the Calogiuri company of Apulia, Italy. The product Vincotto® has been produced by the family since 1825 and is a dark, sweet vinegar made by cooking and reducing the must of 2 varieties of grapes, Negroamaro and Malvasia Nera, for 24 hours. The liquid is then put into oak barrels with the vinegar "mother" (starter) and aged for 4 years to allow it to develop its particular flavor and syrupy consistency.

The taste of Vincotto® resembles fine balsamic vinegar or agridulce, but it is less woody in flavor, with notes of dried fruit and spices. It can be used as a salad seasoning just like a balsamic, and used as a condiment for strongly-flavored foods such as game, roast and cured meats, aged cheeses, and mushroom risotto. It adds a tang to a plain yogurt and makes a good accompaniment to ripe berries, peaches, and figs.

Vincotto® is available commercially in its original, unflavored form called *agrodolce*, as well as flavored with fig, carob, lemon, orange, raspberry, or chili pepper.

AT-A-GLANCE INFO

ACID CONTENT: 5 percent

ALTERNATIVE: Fig vinegar, balsamic vinegar, agridulce

STORAGE: Keep well sealed, out of direct sunlight, preferably in the cool, for up to 2 years or more but always check the manufacturer's use by date.

RECOMMENDED: *Agrodolce* or flavored varieties

VINAGRE AGRIDULCE

Agridulce de Chardonnay vinegar

Agridulce de Cabernet Sauvignon vinegar

Relatively new on the culinary scene outside its native country of Spain, the direct translation of this vinegar is "bittersweet vinegar." It is being marketed as a competitor in the same niche of the market that the Italian balsamics have made for themselves. It is hoped that agridulce will become subject to an appellation standard of control and thus be regulated and protected during its manufacture and sale.

At the moment agridulce is being produced in wineries (bodegas) all over Spain, in different ways, using different wines. The basic production technique involves blending a grape must (mosto) with a partially acidulated wine from the previous year. This is then allowed to acidify slowly for a few months before being transferred to age in oak and chestnut barrels for a few months or longer until the desired level of sweet/sour flavor is achieved.

Use as a seasoning for drizzling over roasted sweet vegetables like tomatoes, red onions, zucchini, bell peppers, eggplant, and squash. Season a paella or drip over broiled or barbecued white fish—delicious with a fish carpaccio. Use to enhance Oriental sweet and sour dishes, or with ripe berries and sweet fruit desserts. It is particularly delicious served with Spanish sheep's and goat's cheeses, and to lighten a rich game dish or a mutton or goat stew.

AT-A-GLANCE INFO

ALTERNATIVE: Vincotto®, fig vinegar, balsamic vinegar

STORAGE: Keep well sealed, out of direct sunlight, preferably in the cool, for up to 2 years or more but always check manufacturer's use by date.

RECOMMENDED: Forvum Cabernet Sauvignon

VERJUICE

Maggie Beer Verjuice

Not strictly a vinegar as the base mixture is unfermented, but it has been used as a souring agent for hundreds of years and is enjoying a bit of a comeback. Verjuice is unfermented grape juice made from unripe green grapes—its name literally means "green juice." It has a tartness like sour apples, rather than the sharp, acidic note of lemon juice or vinegar.

In countries where Islamic law forbids the making of alcohol, verjuice is used as the souring agent of choice. In Iran it is known as *abghooreh* while in the Lebanon it is known as *hosrum*. Other names are Verjus in France, Agresto in Italy, and Agraz in Germany and Spain.

Verjuice has a long culinary history, dating back to Roman times. Today, in California, some wineries have started to make verjuice from red grapes. The French variety is more acidic and is used commercially in the making of mustards like Dijon and Bordeaux.

In the kitchen, use it when you would like the tartness of lemon or vinegar without the harsh edge of either. For the real foodie and wine connoisseur, a salad dressed with a vinegar-based dressing will clash with the wine being drunk at the meal because of the acetic acid content. Using verjuice in the dressing will avoid a conflict of flavors.

AT-A-GLANCE INFO

ALTERNATIVE: Sour apple juice or fresh lemon juice

STORAGE: Store in a cool dark place for up to 10 years, but once opened, keep in the refrigerator and consume by the manufacturer's use by date.

RECOMMENDED: Sangiovese Verjuice, Oh! Legumes Oublies Verjus or Maggie Beer Verjuice

VINAIGRE D'ORLÉANS

Martin Pouret red wine vinegar

Orléans has long been the French vinegar capital. Dating back to the Middle Ages, wines produced nearby were transported to the city in barrels by boat on the river Loire. Because the wine quality wasn't always that good, and the transportation method was slow, by the time they reached their destination, the wines had turned to vinegar. The *Corporation of Vinaigriers, Buffetiers, Sauciers, and Moutardiers Orléans* was founded in 1394 and Orléans vinegars quickly gained a good reputation for their fine flavor and finesse; they were considered the best vinegars in the country. Production was increased and the vinegar was exported all over the world from the Netherlands to America and even to India. In 1594, the wine vinegar was recognized by Henry IV, the King of France, and by the 18th century, the city of Orléans had no fewer than 300 producers.

The discovery by Louis Pasteur of the bacteria *mycoderma aceti* led to great change and a decline in the production of the vinegar by traditional methods. His discovery showed the way for the development of a vinegar-making method that permitted the fermentation process to be speeded up: instead of 3 weeks, vinegar could be produced in huge

AT-A-GLANCE INFO

ALTERNATIVE: White wine vinegar

STORAGE: Keep well sealed, out of direct sunlight, preferably in the cool. Should keep indefinitely but always check manufacturer's use by date.

RECOMMENDED: Try Martin Pouret Vinaigre d'Orléans.

The capital of vinegar, Orléans on the Loire river in France

quantities in less than 24 hours. Today, only the company Maison Martin Pouret, founded in 1797, continues to produce vinegar prepared using the traditional accrual method called "Orléans" from wines of the Loire valley or south-west France (see page 101 for further information on Vinegar Production).

Up until 1965, Martin Pouret only sold its vinegar to the makers of Maille mustard, however, Maille decided to start making and using its own vinegar and they bought out another vinegar maker in Orléans, called Dessaux. To keep the business going, Martin Pouret was forced to sell its vinegar direct to the public as a brand in its own right.

Martin Pouret's descendant of 6 generations, Jean Françoise Martin, now runs the company and is heir and guardian of the traditional techniques. His vinegar bottles proudly bear the phrase "Vinegar according to the old process of Orléans" on the labels. The vinegars are produced from top quality French wines, which are allowed to naturally ferment in oak barrels for 3 weeks, slowly transforming them into vinegar. They are then drawn off and left to mature for 6 months in oak barrels to develop their flavors. After this time they are filtered and bottled. The resulting vinegars are clear, fresh, and perfumed with subtle acidity and no bitterness. Orléans vinegar has the reputation of acting as a *digestif*, helping with the digestion of fatty foods.

Maison Martin Pouret produces many vinegars from white and red wines made from different grapes such as Muscadet, Cabernet, and Chardonnay. They also produce cider vinegar from Normandy cider and many flavored varieties using fruit, herbs, and spices, and the traditional tarragon vinegar. There are also some rare 5 year and 7 year aged vinegars produced for the real gastronome and vinegar connoisseur.

SHERRY VINEGAR

Clovis Sherry Vinegar Reserva

This vinegar is as highly regarded in Spain as balsamic is in Italy, with some top quality varieties being more expensive than sherry itself. It can only be made from sherry wines produced in and around the town of Jerez de la Frontera, Andalucia, south-west Spain, and has its own Denomination of Origin (DO); it is recognized as unique under Spanish and EU law. Production and quality are strictly controlled and monitored by the Consejo Regulador.

The vinegar is made only from the sherry grape must or the young sherry wine produced from the Palomino, Pedro Ximenez, or Moscatel grapes grown in vineyards within the DO "Jerez-Xérès-Sherry;" it contains no residual sugar. Like sherry wine and balsamic vinegar, sherry vinegar is aged in the same way, using the *solera* system. This is a fractional blending system developed in the 19th century, which typically involves 3 or

AT-A-GLANCE INFO

ACID CONTENT: 7–10 percent

ALTERNATIVE: Balsamic or brown rice vinegar plus sugar or honey

STORAGE: Keep well sealed, out of direct sunlight, preferably in the cool. Should keep indefinitely but always check manufacturer's use by date.

RECOMMENDED: Try Rey Fernando de Castilla "La Bodega" Reserva (aged 20 years) - bottled without filtration to preserve the flavours. For a good everyday sherry wine vinegar try "Vinagre Superior" Vinagre de Jerez by A.R. Valdespino, or Clovis Sherry Vinegar "Reserva."

SHERRY VINEGAR

Vintage Superior Sherry wine vinegar

4 tiers of barrels called *criadera*. Vinegar for bottling is siphoned off from the tier nearest the ground or *solera*. These barrels are then filled with vinegar from the *criadera* above. The process continues until the highest *criadera* is topped up with wine from the most recent harvest.

The quality of the vinegar depends on the wine it's made from: good wine turns to good vinegar and thus commands the highest price. The older the vinegar, the better and more intense the flavor. Under the regulations of the DO, "Vinagre de Jerez" must be aged for a minimum of 6 months. "Vinagre de Jerez Reserva" must be aged for at least 2 years but it can be aged for 30 to 50 years. Vinegars labelled "*al Pedro Ximénez*" (often abbreviated to *PX*) are either made from the sweet PX wine or are sweetened by the addition of PX wine. Little sherry vinegar is made from *Moscatel* grapes.

The lengthy process involved in making sherry vinegar and its extended contact with wood means that the resulting vinegar becomes concentrated by natural evaporation and absorbs savory amino acids from wood and microbes; this gives it an assertive yet smooth flavor, a deliciously sweet, nutty aroma, and deep brownish red color. Regulations stipulate a minimum 7 degrees of acidity but some of the older varieties can reach 10 percent or more.

A traditional ingredient in authentic Spanish cooking, sherry vinegar is often the preferred vinegar of choice of some of the world's best chefs. It is used to add flavor to sauces and marinades and is an excellent agent for deglazing a pan after cooking rich meats like duck, beef, or game. Sherry vinegar is not as intense as balsamic, but it does add a distinctly different flavor to dressings and can be used sprinkled directly onto hot vegetable dishes.

APPLE CIDER VINEGAR

Waitrose cider vinegar

Vinaigre de cidre de Normandie

Apple cider vinegar, otherwise known simply as cider vinegar, has long been a specialty of the apple-growing areas in north-east America and parts of Europe, especially Normandy in France and south-west England.

The color of cider vinegar varies from a warm, pale honey-like shade to dark yellowish brown depending on the variety and quality, and it can be clear or cloudy. The flavor is sharp and strong if used at full strength and tastes very acidic, therefore it is best diluted. Good quality vinegars, once diluted, often reveal a soft, almost perfumed, appley taste.

Clear cider vinegar has been pasteurized and is the variety most commonly seen in the grocery store. It is filtered to remove impurities and is most used in the kitchen. The cloudy variety is unfiltered and organic, and there is a growing belief that this type of cider vinegar has health benefits.

In the kitchen, cider vinegar is traditionally used for chutney making and pickling orchard fruits such as quince, pears, and apples, and is usually sweetened and lightly spiced with cinnamon and cloves. It also makes a good base vinegar to be flavored with herbs.

AT-A-GLANCE INFO

ACID CONTENT: 5 percent

ALTERNATIVE: For pickling: malt or white wine vinegar; for other use, white wine vinegar

STORAGE: Keep well sealed, out of direct sunlight, preferably in the cool. Should keep indefinitely but always check use by date.

RECOMMENDED: Aspall's Organic Cyder vinegar

WARNING: Cider vinegar is extremely caustic if taken undiluted. If you have an acid-sensitive digestive system, it is better to take cider vinegar for health benefits in a gentler form such as dried powder or capsules.

PERRY VINEGAR

Pear vinegar

ACETO DI MELE

Kuhne Exquisit apple vinegar

Made in the same way as cider vinegar, using perry wine (fermented pear juice) as the base. The vinegar is pale amber in color with a mildly acidic flavor with a hint of fresh pear. Use it in dressings and vinaigrettes, particularly those containing fresh pear in order to accentuate their natural sweet flavor.

Perry vinegar should not to be confused with pear vinegar which is likely to be a white wine vinegar infused with fresh pear (see fruit vinegars page 145).

Made solely from the extraction and natural fermentation of the juice obtained from good quality Italian apples. Apple vinegar has become popular as a health product and is believed to have energizing properties; it is particularly beneficial for those suffering from lethargy.

Light golden in color with 5 percent acidity, apple vinegar has a fragrant apple aroma and a fresh tart flavor. It is commonly used in everyday Italian cooking, taking the edge off rich and creamy sauces or adding a "bite" to soups and pasta dishes.

AT-A-GLANCE INFO

ALTERNATIVE: Cider vinegar

STORAGE: Keep well sealed, out of direct sunlight. Should keep indefinitely but always check manufacturer's use by date.

RECOMMENDED: Crone's Organic Perry Vinegar

AT-A-GLANCE INFO

ALTERNATIVE: Other fruit vinegar or cider vinegar

STORAGE: Keep well sealed, out of direct sunlight, preferably in the cool. Should keep indefinitely but always check use by date.

RECOMMENDED: Kuhne Exquisit Aceto di Mele

RAISIN (OR GRAPE) VINEGAR

Vinegar made from raisins is a popular ingredient throughout the Middle East. It is known as *Khal 'anab* in Arabic. This cloudy mid-brown colored vinegar is traditionally produced in Turkey (Sultan is a leading brand), but it is also made in Greece. It has a pleasant fruity but mildly acidic taste, and is often infused with cinnamon to add more depth of flavor.

It is most frequently used in vinaigrette-style salad dressings, and also goes well with the flavors of raw sweet tomatoes, grated carrot, dried fruit salads, and broiled eggplant.

AT-A-GLANCE INFO

ALTERNATIVE: Sherry vinegar, balsamic vinegar or date vinegar

STORAGE: Keep well sealed, out of direct sunlight, preferably in the cool. Should keep indefinitely but always check the use by date.

RECOMMENDED: Try the Sultan brand or Fersan raisin vinegar.

DATE VINEGAR

The Babylonians were making this vinegar as long ago as 5000 BC, and the Romans carried on the tradition. Nowadays it is used all over the Middle East, but is particularly popular in Iran. Date vinegar is made from the juice of dates (see facing page), which is fermented in alcohol. A starter is added and it's then allowed to stand in order to convert into vinegar.

The mild, slightly sweet flavor goes well with sweet salad ingredients, and makes an interesting dressing for sweet strawberries.

AT-A-GLANCE INFO

ACID CONTENT: Info from bottle

ALTERNATIVE: Sherry vinegar, balsamic vinegar or raisin vinegar

STORAGE: Keep well sealed, out of direct sunlight, preferably in the cool. Always check manufacturer's use by date.

RECOMMENDED: Mahram date vinegar

COCONUT VINEGAR

UFC CoCo vinegar

As well as coconut palm being used to make vinegar, the coconut milk or water from inside the coconut shell is also used. The coconut water is filtered, sugar is added, and then it is brought to boiling point to pasteurize it. After this, it is cooled, and yeast is added. It is left to ferment for a week, then the liquid is siphoned off and a starter culture is added. It is fermented for another week before ageing and bottling. This gives a low-acid vinegar of approximately 4 percent that is cloudy and sweet compared to other vinegars.

As with the palm vinegars mentioned above, this is very popular in Pacific countries, and is really catching on right now in Australia where it is being incorporated into homespun recipes, giving an exotic twist to local ingredients.

AT-A-GLANCE INFO

ACID CONTENT: 4 percent

ALTERNATIVE: Cane vinegar or 3 parts white wine or cider vinegar to 1 part water

STORAGE: Keep well sealed, out of direct sunlight, preferably in the cool. Should keep indefinitely but always check manufacturer's use by date.

RECOMMENDED: Try UFC Coco Vinegar or Datu Pitu Natural Coconut Vinegar.

SUGAR PALM OR ARENGA VINEGAR

UFC Native vinegar

This vinegar is made from a variety of sugar palm tree (*Arenga pinnata*) called *kaong* or *irok* in the Philippines. The trees required for the process need to be established in growth, usually 10 to 15 years old. The vinegar is made from the sap of the male flowering stalks. The trees can be wild or cultivated, and the blooms take a few months to develop. Once opened, the flowers are cut and tapped. The cut will produce sweet sap in the morning, which will turn sour by the end of the day. The sap is collected manually by climbing the trees, and it has to be collected every day in order for production to be continuous. The sap is put into clay pots (*burnay* jars), covered in cheesecloth, and allowed to ferment for 3 to 4 weeks. Coconut leaves are put over the jars to shield them from the excess heat of the sun. The resulting mixture is aged in about 8 weeks, then bottled as it is with nothing else added.

This vinegar used to be made locally for household consumption, but now it is made commercially on a small scale. It is sold in frosted bottles. There are two versions—one is straight up, with a sweet-sour taste, the other has rosemary steeped in it. It is used like the coconut palm vinegars (see page 126).

AT-A-GLANCE INFO

ALTERNATIVE: Palm (coconut), coconut or cane vinegar, or 3 parts white wine or cider vinegar to 1 part water

STORAGE: Keep well sealed, out of direct sunlight, preferably in the cool, for up to 2 years or more but always check manufacturer's use by date.

RECOMMENDED: Try UFC Native Palm Leaf Vinegar.

BEER VINEGAR

Beer making is a serious business in Europe, especially in Germany where there is a Law of Purity for beer that dates back to 1516. Just as there are many different types of beer, there are also several varieties of vinegar made from them. Vinegar made from beer is produced in Germany, Austria, and the Netherlands, where it is used as a popular seasoning. Although the flavor and depth of color depends on the type of beer from which it is made, in general, beer vinegars usually have a varying degree of malt flavor with a sharp acidic note and range from light to rich gold in color.

The first original beer vinegar made in Bavaria was produced by the Burkhardt company. It is a light golden color, with a sharp and not overly complex flavor. It has definite beer aromas and a light malty taste. Rattenburg is made on a small scale in the Tyrolean village of the same name. It is richly golden in color with a mellow beer flavor.

Beer vinegar lends itself well to strong flavors and hearty meat dishes. It is also a popular condiment for dipping strong cheese. It is ideal with sausages and meat platters, and blends well with a strong mustard to make a thick vinaigrette or with caramelized onions in a cream sauce.

AT-A-GLANCE INFO

ALTERNATIVE: Cider vinegar

STORAGE: Most beer vinegars are packaged in glass casket-type jars with resealable stoppers. They keep well in a cool place for up to 2 years.

RECOMMENDED: Bavarian beer vinegar, Burkhardt or Austrian beer vinegar Rattenberg.

PALM (COCONUT) VINEGAR

In southern and western Asian regions, vinegar is less depended upon as a souring agent, as lime juice, tamarind, and other sour fruits are used instead. However there are some vinegars worthy of note from this region, mostly derived from the coconut and sugar palms (see facing page). Perhaps the most common vinegar in South-east Asia and the Pacific, particularly favored in the Philippines, is palm vinegar known natively as *sukang paombong* or *sukang niyog*. The vinegar is also popular in parts of southern India and Thailand.

Palm vinegars are white and cloudy. Some are mild, whilst some have a sharp, acidic taste. All have a faint yeasty or musty after-taste. Palm vinegar adds a piquant flavor to the traditional dishes of the region such as *adobo* (a pork or chicken and pork stew served with its spicy sauce or fried crisp), and hot curries, rice, and vegetable dishes. In addition, there are various kinds of dipping sauces, pickles, or *achar*, which are as popular a condiment in this region as salt and pepper are to the western world. With its acidic edge, palm vinegar can be used to replace lemon or lime juice in a recipe, and it is particularly ideal to serve with salty fish as it helps mellow out the intense flavor as well as adding a touch of the exotic.

AT-A-GLANCE INFO

ALTERNATIVE: White rice vinegar or 1 part white wine vinegar, 1 part water, and a squeeze or two of lime juice.

STORAGE: Keep well sealed, out of direct sunlight, preferably in the cool, for up to 2 years or more but always check manufacturer's use by date.

RECOMMENDED: Datu Puti Cane Vinegar (Sukang Maasim)

MALT VINEGAR

Sarsons distilled malt vinegar

Sarsons malt vinegar

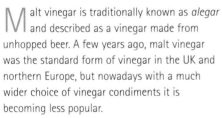

Malt vinegar is traditionally known as *alegar* and described as a vinegar made from unhopped beer. A few years ago, malt vinegar was the standard form of vinegar in the UK and northern Europe, but nowadays with a much wider choice of vinegar condiments it is becoming less popular.

To make malt vinegar, cereal grains and sprouted barley are "malted" causing the starch in the grain to turn to the sugar maltose. This is then brewed into an ale (beer), which in turn is made into vinegar and then aged. The resulting vinegar is naturally light brown in color, however it is usually colored with caramel to make it a richer brown. The flavor is strongly malted, which renders it too robust for dressings and condiments but it is ideal for pickling. It can be used in marinades for red meats, but should be used in small quantities and combined with other ingredients and some sweetness to reduce any overpowering flavors.

Malt vinegar can be flavored with spices like black and white peppercorns, allspice, cloves, root ginger, and hot chilies and is sold as pickling vinegar. It is used to preserve small onions, cucumber, green walnuts, red cabbage, and to make a traditional preserved vegetable chutney called piccalilli.

AT-A-GLANCE INFO

ACID CONTENT: 5 percent

ALTERNATIVE: Beer or cider vinegar

STORAGE: Keep well sealed, out of direct sunlight, preferably in the cool, for up to 2 years or more but always check manufacturer's use by date.

RECOMMENDED: Try Sarson's Malt Vinegar for a really British flavor or Casa Perdido Malt Vinegar.

Casa Perdido malt vinegar

White vinegar

In the UK, malt vinegar may be distilled to concentrate the acetic acid and produce a very strong, clear or "white" vinegar labeled as "spirit" vinegar. This is very harsh and is only really suitable for pickling vegetables where the natural colorings are to be preserved. In the US, distilled vinegar is white vinegar made from distilled alcohol—it is a cheap product used mostly for household jobs like cleaning glass or as a detergent.

In the UK, malt vinegar has a long association with freshly cooked deep-fried potato chips (fries). However, this solution sprinkled liberally over the nation's favorite fast food, is really a cheaper, non-brewed vinegar-type solution made up of synthetically produced acetic acid and caramel coloring. Under the laws of the UK, the US, and some other countries, this product cannot be called "vinegar," and is thus labeled "non-brewed condiment."

RICE VINEGARS

Rice fields

There are many varieties of vinegars made from this highly revered starchy Asian grain and the wine made from it. In the US, rice vinegar generally means Japanese or Japanese-style vinegar. Originating from China, rice vinegars have been made and used for hundreds of years and range in flavor from mild to strong, and from sweet to savory. In general, Chinese vinegars tend to be stronger in flavor than those from Japan, which are usually mild and sweet. Chinese rice vinegars range in color from clear (or white), through to reddish brown and even black, whilst those from Japan are mostly clear or straw-colored. The vinegars are made from whole grains—sometimes roasted—which are fermented using a mold culture and are often aged with extra molds, yeasts, and bacteria which impart their own flavorings to the vinegar mix.

Rice vinegar is a key ingredient in authentic Oriental cooking. Its unique flavor enables it to draw out sweet, salt, and "umami" (monosodium-glutamate-like) flavors, and adds a delicious aroma to any dish it is added to. Rice vinegars are widely used as dipping sauces as well as a cooking ingredient. In western dishes, the vinegars add an interesting tang to marinades and barbecue rubs, as well as livening up dressings and stir-fries.

In general, rice vinegar increases the potency of vitamin C, which is one reason why it's said to be good for the complexion. It contains some calcium and carbohydrates with traces of iron and protein and it also acts as a stimulant to the appetite. Medicinally, it is believed to aid digestion and ease bowel and stomach disorders.

AT-A-GLANCE INFO

ACID CONTENT: 2–4 percent

ALTERNATIVE: For black rice vinegar use balsamic and red rice vinegar plus sugar, or cider or red wine vinegar plus Worcestershire sauce; for red rice vinegar use black rice vinegar, cider or red wine vinegar; for brown rice vinegar use sherry vinegar plus sugar; for white rice vinegar use champagne or white wine vinegar.

STORAGE: Kept in a cool, dry place away from the light, rice vinegars should keep indefinitely, but one should always take note of the use by date on the bottle.

RECOMMENDED: Chinkiang Gold Plum Black Vinegar, Pearl River Bridge or Koon Chung red rice vinegar

CHENCU

The full name of this vinegar is Shanxi Lao Chencu which means mature vinegar. In China, it is one of the 4 most famous kinds of vinegar, along with vinegar from Zhejiang, Sichuan and Fujian provinces. Chencu has been used as a seasoning for over a thousand years and originated in the Shanxi Provence in 770BC. In Shanxi, it is still the custom to take a spoonful of this highly prized vinegar before a meal in order to aid digestion and thus keeping with a tradition recorded in one of the earliest books of historical China.

Shanxi has over 100 vinegar factories, which produce more than 200,000 tons of vinegar annually. The Shanxi vinegar factories between them have developed many other vinegar products to keep up with ever changing market forces.

The best vinegar within the region is said to come from Qingxu County where there is a museum dedicated to the vinegar, containing ancient documents charting the history of Chencu over the years.

It is used as a general seasoning for salads, dips and is particularly good with seafood. Chencu is also used medicinally and is claimed to prevent high blood pressure, hepatitis and skin diseases; it is believed to contain 18 amino acids, as well as minerals such as calcium, iron, zinc and manganese. In China today, Chencu is taken as a health drink by young and old alike and is made into a long, refreshing, soft drink by mixing with soda water.

Chencu is quite difficult to obtain outside China, but you could try Pat Chun's Aged Sourghum Vinegar as an alternative to standard Chinese rice vinegars.

(CHINESE) BLACK VINEGAR

Black vinegar originated in China and spread across much of Asia at the same time as many other foods. It can be made with a wide assortment of ingredients, in many different combinations, so there can be an immense variance in taste. Black vinegar is made by fermenting grain in liquid, which is then allowed to age. The grains used can be rice, wheat, millet, sorghum, or barley and the finished vinegar may contain added sugar, spices, or caramel coloring, so it is worth checking the label if you are looking for a natural flavor.

Black vinegar is most widely used in southern China where it is regarded as a general "season all" staple. Many people prefer black vinegar made from only rice, and one of the most prized varieties is the Chinkiang black vinegar from the city of Zhenjiang—it is made with glutinous rice and malt, giving it a more intense sweetness. Good quality black vinegars are also produced in Tianjin and Hong Kong. A lighter form of black vinegar, made from white and brown rice along with barley, is produced in Japan, where it is called *kurozu*. It is popular in southern Japan, especially in Kagoshima. The vinegar is aged for between 3 and 12 months and is marketed as a healthful tonic since its manufacturers claim that it contains high concentrations of amino acids.

Very dark and inky rich in color, but milder in taste than you might expect, the flavor of Chinese black vinegar is slightly smoky and spicy, but with a sharpness similar to balsamic vinegar, and the texture is slightly thicker than other rice vinegars. Some varieties have a distinctly malty flavor.

There are great differences of flavor between brands, so be prepared to experiment. You should read labels closely, since different grains have different flavors, and some companies sell cheaper versions of black vinegar which lack the complexity of the real thing.

(CHINESE) RED VINEGAR

(CHINESE) WHITE VINEGAR

Traditionally, the distinctive color of this vinegar comes from red yeast rice (also called red fermented rice, red koji rice, or *ang-kak*) which is a bright reddish purple grain, cultivated with the mold *Monascus purpureus*. Dark reddish brown in color, and much less inky than the black variety, red vinegar has a distinctly different flavor—it is both tart and sweet with a definite spicy edge, which is derived from the red mold. Take care when choosing between brands as some manufacturers use artificial coloring and flavoring instead of the traditional red rice and mold combination. Hong Kong is reputed to make some of the best red vinegars.

Red vinegar is usually used as a dipping sauce, or sprinkled over noodle dishes and it makes an excellent accompaniment to seafood. It is often added to soups, in particular Hot and Sour and Shark's Fin soup obtain their piquancy from this flavoring.

A colorless rice vinegar, that is more like regular vinegars than either black or red varieties, yet is less acidic and milder in flavor. It is also the most similar Chinese rice vinegar to Japanese varieties. White rice vinegar is clear and has the slightly sweet taste of glutinous rice. It is used in sweet and sour sauces, for pickling, and for seasoning stir-fries where the color of the other ingredients needs to be preserved. It is widely used across the whole of eastern Asia.

Gourmet or aged vinegars are also available, usually made in Taiwan. Although twice as expensive as regular white vinegar, the flavor is more sophisticated and this makes it the superior choice for dipping or dressings.

JAPANESE RICE VINEGARS

Brown rice vinegar

Rice vinegar was brought from China and taken to Japan in the 4th century A.D., at about the same time that the closely related process for making rice wine (*sake*) was introduced. Natural rice vinegar maintained its popularity in Japan until the early 1900s when a cheaper alcohol-based vinegar brewing method was developed. Japanese vinegar (*zu* or *su*) is much milder, mellower, and sweeter than other rice vinegars, and is regarded as an altogether more refined product. Colors range from clear to straw yellow. There are 2 distinct varieties: the traditional vinegar which is made from fermented brown rice, and a seasoning vinegar called *awasezu* which is made by adding rice vinegar to *sake* along with salt and sugar.

Natural Japanese brown rice vinegar is considered a very healthy food in Japan and is served with almost every meal. It is made with cooked brown rice, a small amount of seed vinegar from a previous batch, and water. These ingredients are allowed to ferment together

AT-A-GLANCE INFO

Acid content: 2–4 percent

Alternative: Per $\frac{1}{2}$ cup white rice vinegar, add 1 tablespoon white sugar and 3/4 teaspoon of salt. Sometimes a small piece of kombu seaweed is added for extra flavor. This mixture will keep stored in the refrigerator for several weeks in a covered container.

Storage: Follow manufacturer's instructions

Recommended: Nachi Kurokomesu (Kurozu) Sweet Brown Rice Vinegar is long aged and considered one of the finest brands.

Yutaka Japanese rice vinegar

for about 8 months. This combination gives a refreshing and versatile seasoning, full-bodied without the sharpness usually associated with vinegar. In cooking, brown rice vinegar helps to balance salt and adds interest to a recipe by providing a stimulating contrast of flavors. Top-grade varieties are made in small batches and are brewed in clay jars.

When choosing a brand, amber glass bottles help preserve delicate flavors, aromas, and nutrients. Read the label to check for authenticity as many commercial vinegars contain synthetic products made from glacial acetic acid, a petroleum product. Others are made from alcohol produced for industrial use and any vinegar labeled "distilled," is potentially a highly-refined chemical-based product. The very finest Japanese rice vinegar is called *genmai mochigome su*, and is made from unpolished glutinous rice.

Use brown rice vinegar sprinkled over salads for *sunomono* (vinegared salad) or cooked vegetables and grains. It is the essential seasoning for *sushi*, sometimes called the sandwich of Japan. This delicacy consists of cooked rice sprinkled with a dressing of vinegar, salt, and sugar, called *sushi-zu*. The dressing adds a glossy sheen to the rice and the longer it is left, the greater the flavor that is imparted. The rice is then shaped in small bundles and wrapped in fish or seaweed. For convenience, you can buy *sushi-zu* in ready-made form sold as Seasoned Rice Vinegar—Mitsukan is a well-known brand—however, a Japanese food purist would turn their nose up at such a product, which often contains sugary syrups, MSG, and other flavorings. Another type of sweet Japanese rice vinegar called *yamabukusu* is also used for seasoning rice.

CANE (ILOCOS) VINEGAR

Datu Puti cane vinegar

Sukang Maasim

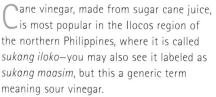

Cane vinegar, made from sugar cane juice, is most popular in the Ilocos region of the northern Philippines, where it is called *sukang iloko*—you may also see it labeled as *sukang maasim*, but this a generic term meaning sour vinegar.

If you buy cane vinegar expecting a sweet flavor, you will be disappointed. Little or none of the residual sugar remains in the product and as a result, it has a mild, mellow taste, slightly malty, but with a note of freshness. It is often compared to rice vinegar, and can range in color from dark yellow to golden brown. A dark, pungent version is made in the Philippines flavored with *samak* or *Macaranga* leaf. It is used as an ingredient in local meat dishes and sausages, as well as for medicinal purposes as a disinfectant or coolant for fevers. This vinegar is more like a strong balsamic vinegar.

Cane vinegar is used in many sauces and marinades, particularly in pepper-based hot sauces. It also shows up as a frequent ingredient in teriyaki-type marinades. Cane vinegar is a relatively flexible ingredient and can be used in place of other vinegars when a slightly milder flavor is required.

AT-A-GLANCE INFO

ALTERNATIVE: Palm (coconut), palm (sugar), or coconut vinegar, or 3 parts white wine or cider vinegar to 1 part water

STORAGE: Cane vinegar ages and keeps well. Store at room temperature for up to 2 years.

RECOMMENDED: Try Steen's Cane Vinegar from Louisiana, or Datu Puti Sukang Iloko Sugar Cane Vinegar.

HONEY VINEGAR

This is a rare vinegar, traditionally made in the French household (*Vinaigre de miel*) using a method dating back hundreds of years. Today it is also produced commercially in France, Corsica, and Italy.

Made purely from water and honey, honey vinegar takes 12 months to make—6 months to reach fermentation (when it becomes mead—honey wine) and a further 6 months to turn into vinegar. It is made and aged in oak barrels, and the resulting vinegar is mildly acidic (approximately 5 degrees or lower) with a light perfumed flavor and fragrant aroma. The color varies from clear light gold to rich gold, depending on the area where it is produced.

It is ideally used to season light vinaigrettes and dressings for herb and flower salads, chicken, and seafood. Best used with other mild flavors to enjoy its exquisite taste.

AT-A-GLANCE INFO

ACID CONTENT: 5 percent or below

ALTERNATIVE: Champagne vinegar plus a little strong flavored honey

STORAGE: Follow manufacturer's instructions

RECOMMENDED: Try Vinaigre de Miel a l'Ancienne, a pale straw-coloured French honey vinegar or darker Corsican honey vinegars.

WHEY VINEGAR

Whey is a watery by-product obtained during cheese manufacturing. Cheese is produced from about 10 percent of milk solids, and the remaining 90 percent forms a thin, cloudy liquid called whey. Whey has a high nutrient content of protein, lactose, vitamins, and minerals.

Whey vinegar is produced in Switzerland and to a lesser extent in New Zealand. The whey is first made alcoholic by adding a yeast such as *kluyveromyces fragilis* to aid fermentation. Once it has become alcoholic, a starter culture such as *acetobacter pasteurianus* is added to convert the alcohol to acetic acid and thus into vinegar. The resulting product is amber in color with a faint odor of cow's milk and a mellow acidity and slightly cheesy taste.

It is considered a health tonic as it is said to aid digestion and is often called "dietary vinegar." It has a distinctive taste that does not lend itself as an obvious choice for a salad dressing. It is considered a dairy product under Jewish kosher laws.

AT-A-GLANCE INFO

ACID CONTENT: 5–6 percent

ALTERNATIVE: Strong, distinctive taste—no obvious alternative.

YUZU ZU (YUZU SU)

Yuzu is a citrus fruit grown primarily in Japan (see facing page). The yuzu tree grows wild in Tibet and Central China, but since its introduction over a thousand years ago, it is most popular in Japan where it is cultivated. Japanese immigrants recently brought the trees to the US, and the yuzu is now also being cultivated in California. Depending on the variety, the rind of the fruit can be orangey yellow or green (often referred to as a yuzu lime). Some varieties have an extremely thick rind and almost no pulp; others have a thinner rind and more pulp. On average 1 yuzu yields about 1 teaspoon of juice.

The juice has an exotic, tart/sweet flavor with hints of lime, tangerine, and pine. It is very acidic with a clean, fresh aroma; it is also rich in vitamin C. Yuzu zu is a rich, gold-colored vinegar made from a blend of the juice with brown rice wine vinegar; this gives the vinegar a citrus, refreshing taste.

In cooking, add a few drops of yuzu zu in the same way as you would add other vinegars to dress salads, or sprinkle on sushi. Add to carbonated mineral water with sugar syrup to make a refreshing drink or try chilling it and using as a dip or dressing for a cold seafood dish.

AT-A-GLANCE INFO

ACID CONTENT: Info from bottle

ALTERNATIVE: White rice wine vinegar with a few drops of lime juice added.

STORAGE: Info from bottle

RECOMMENDED: Try Mitoku Yuzu Vinegar made by the Komatsu Yuzusui Company or O Olive Oil California Yuzu Rice Vinegar.

SUKA VINEGAR

KOMBUCHA VINEGAR

Another vinegar from the coconut palm is the suka variety, called *suka bisaya* or native vinegar, in the Philippines. It is made from the sap of coconut palm tree flowers. It is not very acidic and so has more of a sweet edge to it. Once gathered, the sap is allowed to ferment naturally for about 3 weeks. For the first 2 weeks, it's known as *bahal*, and is very alcoholic and sour and can be drunk at this stage as a beverage. After a further 3 weeks, it is filtered, pasteurized, and bottled.

Suka vinegar can be used on its own as a condiment, or as a flavoring ingredient in local dishes like palm vinegar.

Also referred to as "probiotic" vinegar, this vinegar is made from kombucha (see facing page), a symbiotic culture of yeast and bacteria, which is most familiarly brewed and taken as a sweetened tea or tisane. Normally kombucha is brewed at home for between 6 and 8 days after which time it has a refreshing semi-sweet, slightly sparkling apple cider taste. Longer aging of 8 to 14 days (or sometimes longer) produces a sharper more vinegar-like taste. During fermentation, a complex array of nutrients are produced and the vinegar becomes populated with bacteria which some claim can promote a healthy digestive tract, though scientific studies are inconclusive.

In Chinese folk medicine, the vinegar is a medicine in its own right, treating a wide range of disorders and complaints, including gynaecological, dermatological, and trauma conditions.

In the kitchen, kombucha vinegar is primarily used to make a vinaigrette for leaf or fruit salads and salsas. The brew can be enhanced by adding strawberries, blackberries, or blueberries at the beginning of fermentation to add extra flavor and fruitiness. Fresh mint or ginger root can be used to give an uplifting edge.

AT-A-GLANCE INFO

ACID CONTENT: Info from bottle

ALTERNATIVE: Palm (coconut), palm (sugar), or coconut vinegar, or 3 parts white wine or cider vinegar to 1 part water

STORAGE: Info from bottle

RECOMMENDED: Mama Sita Coconut Vinegar made from coconut nectar or Wilderness Family Coconut Vinegar with Honey, an organic filtered vinegar made from the sap of coconut flowers—there is also an unfiltered version.

AT-A-GLANCE INFO

ACID CONTENT: Info from bottle

ALTERNATIVE: Cider vinegar or ume zu

STORAGE: Keep refrigerated or in a cool place and follow instructions given with starter culture for usage instructions.

RECOMMENDED: Starter culture for making your own is available from specialist suppliers.

MAPLE VINEGAR

Maple syrup production has been an essential part of Canadian food history for hundreds of years. Early colonists were taught how to tap the trunks of the black maple tree by the native Indian population in order to obtain the sap, which is evaporated to make syrup or sugar. Today, the trees grow in south-east Canada and the north-east states of America. Wherever the syrup is made, it is most likely that other products such as vinegar are made as well.

The prime time for collecting maple sap (by collecting it in buckets fixed to the trees) for syrup making is from the end of February/beginning of March until mid-April. After this time, the sap loses much of its sweetness and becomes watery; when boiled down it will not make sugar, but is used instead to make vinegar.

Production of maple vinegar is similar to the process used to make cane vinegar (see page 136). The watery syrup is simmered down to a light syrup, and then this syrup is fermented into vinegar. It is then aged in oak barrels.

Maple vinegar is richly golden in color—not unlike the syrup—but it is not sweet. Instead it has an earthy flavor with a hint of spice and the merest hint of sweetness. It makes a great dressing for smoked salmon and trout, or char-broiled vegetable salads; try adding it to barbecue marinades and sauces to enhance the smokiness of the cooked food.

AT-A-GLANCE INFO

ACID CONTENT: Info from bottle

ALTERNATIVE: Sherry vinegar with a touch of maple syrup

STORAGE: Info from bottle

RECOMMENDED: Try Cuisine Perel's Spicy Pecan Vinegar or Boyajannic Pure Vermont Maple Vinegar.

HERB AND SPICE VINEGARS

Maille wine vinegar with tarragon

Vinaigre Saveur Menthe Verte

Made in the same way as fruit-flavored vinegars by adding herbs or spices directly to cider, wine, or rice vinegar and then maturing for some time to allow the flavors to develop.

Tarragon vinegar is the most well known of all herb vinegars. Since the flavor of tarragon doesn't survive drying, using the fresh herb to flavor vinegar is a way to deliver that distinctive taste when fresh tarragon is not available.

Herbes de Provence is another popular herb blend used to flavor white wine vinegar. Other herbs you may come across are basil, lavender, mint, oregano, rose petal, thyme, and rosemary.

For spice vinegars, garlic is a widely available flavor, and the vinegar offers a more subtle, savory, garlicky hit in a dressing or marinade than using a fresh clove. Peppercorns and nutmeg are added to vinegars to give warmth and a slight earthy edge, as well as root ginger, cardamom, cloves, chiles, cinnamon, and even whole vanilla beans and lemon grass.

Herb and spice vinegars are easy to make at home; just put 1 or 2 washed and slightly bruised herb sprigs in a bottle of lightly warmed vinegar, seal tightly, and let it stand for a few days, shaking it gently every day.

AT-A-GLANCE INFO

ACID CONTENT: 5-6 percent

ALTERNATIVE: White wine or cider vinegar plus fresh herb or spice

STORAGE: Keep well sealed, out of direct sunlight, preferably in the cool, for up to 2 years or more but always check manufacturer's use by date.

RECOMMENDED: Try J Leblanc Tarragon Vinegar or Clovis Tarragon White Wine Vinegar.

VEGETABLE VINEGARS

Fischerauer Karotten Essig

These are not as familiar as fruit vinegars and are a bit more expensive, but definitely worth investigating. Vegetable vinegars are the ultimate accompaniment to vegetable dishes and salads, and marry very well with nut and seed oils (see page 148 for pairing suggestions).

Made in the same way as natural fruit vinegars by fermenting the extracted and pressed vegetable juice, vegetable vinegars are produced in Italy and Germany and usually have distinctive flavors and colors. Here are some typical flavors:

Beetroot vinegar—robust, earthy flavor and dark pink color; goes well with red vegetable salads and rich meats.

Capsicum vinegar—made from green bell peppers and has a pale golden color and rich, fresh flavor; perfect with all salad vegetables, particularly where raw bell peppers are added.

Carrot vinegar—slightly sweet, intense vegetable flavor and light golden-orange color; excellent for dressing lightly steamed spring vegetables or adding extra tang to a creamy carrot soup.

Cucumber vinegar—intensely refreshing cucumber flavor, pale golden color, the best choice for dressing a crisp salad with fresh herbs or smoked fish, even sushi.

Jerusalem artichoke vinegar—produced on a small scale in Germany, this is a very interesting sounding vinegar, earthy-flavored, and earthy-colored; recommended for dressing root vegetable salads.

Tomato vinegar—pale golden in color and tasting like unsweetened tomato ketchup, it is an obvious choice for dressing tomato-based sauces, soups, and salads.

AT-A-GLANCE INFO

ACID CONTENT: Various

ALTERNATIVE: White wine vinegar plus vegetable juice

STORAGE: Keep well sealed, out of direct sunlight, preferably in the cool, for up to 2 years or more but always check manufacturer's use by date.

RECOMMENDED: Try Luggin Beetroot Vinegar, Pommer Capsicum Vinegar, or Fischeraueur carrot, cucumber, or tomato vinegars; also A l'Olivier Tomato vinegar.

FRUIT VINEGARS

There are 2 types of fruit vinegar: the more expensive vinegar made naturally from fermented fruit juice, which is then made into an alcoholic liquid and later turned into vinegar; or, more commonly, fruit-flavored wine or cider vinegar where fruit has been steeped in a base vinegar to flavor and color it. The flavor possibilities of the latter are infinite with examples ranging from the common apple, pear, or raspberry to the more exotic passion fruit, pomegranate, chokecherry, or saskatoon berry. Inferior fruit vinegars may be made adding sweetened fruit syrups, color, and flavorings to a base vinegar, so always check the label if you are looking for an authentic product.

Most naturally fermented fruit juice vinegars are produced in Europe, where there is a growing market for high price gourmet ingredients made solely from a specific type of fruit. Blueberry vinegar is a specialty of the Valle d'Aosta in Italy and is made from fermenting blueberries into alcohol. Vinegar starter is added to this alcohol to turn it into vinegar. The resulting mix is deep purplish blue in color with a fragrant, sweet aroma, and a pleasant, mildly sweet berry taste (Note: a cheaper version is most often available commercially and is made by soaking blueberries in cider vinegar). Blueberry vinegar is best served drizzled over blue cheeses, creamy goat's cheese, with melon, or over strawberries. It can also be served dripped over creamy mascarpone or ricotta cheese accompanied by a few fresh berries as a simple, yet refreshing dessert.

Fig vinegar is another specialty fruit vinegar, which offers a product not dissimilar to a balsamic. It is sweet and tart at the same time, and richly brown in color. Lovely for deglazing a pan after cooking duck or other game meats, and perfect for drizzling over sweet fresh figs with a dollop of soft cheese or thick yogurt. Try Delouis of France Fig Bouquet. Other natural quality fruit vinegar

Lemon vinegar

AT-A-GLANCE INFO

ACID CONTENT: Info from bottle

ALTERNATIVE: White wine vinegar plus fruit juice and sugar or honey

STORAGE: Keep well sealed, out of direct sunlight, preferably in the cool, for up to 2 years or more but always check manufacturer's use by date.

RECOMMENDED: Try Douce Vallee Aceto di Mirtilli (blueberry) and Aceto di Lamponi (raspberry), or Delouis of France Fig Bouquet. Also A l'Olivier Passion Fruit, Raspberry, or Fig Vinegars or Cuisine Perel's Blood Orange Vinegar.

Clearspring Japanese ume plum seasoning

These beverages are a particular hit with the fashion-conscious young men and women of the Japanese cities, with bars selling fruit vinegars opening up all over the country, especially in Tokyo.

There is a wide range of fruit-flavored vinegars available on the market. The best ones are made using a good quality wine or cider vinegar in which the chosen fruit is macerated for up to 6 weeks in mildly warm conditions. The resulting vinegar should be pleasantly aromatic, freshly colored, and fruity tasting, with a natural sweetness depending on the fruit used. There may possibly be sediment in the base of the bottle depending on how finely filtered the product has been—some vinegars are bottled with whole fruit in them and this in time will mature farther, deepening the color and flavor of the vinegar. The world is your oyster when it comes to fruits used and they are often complemented by additional herbs and spices—try grapefruit and lavender or lemon and basil.

This type of fruit vinegar is easy enough to make at home, but use a trustworthy recipe. If too much fruit is added to a vinegar, it may not be sufficiently acidic to prevent harmful bacteria developing (see page150 for a classic berry vinegar recipe).

flavors to try would be blackcurrant, fig, peach, plum, prune, or quince.

Beyond Europe, natural fruit vinegars are used, but to a lesser extent. Persimmon vinegar is popular in South Korea, and a jujube vinegar is produced in China. In Mexico, pineapple vinegar is used to dress spicy flavored salads and salsas; it is reputedly very good but it is difficult to obtain elsewhere and is usually made in the home. In Japan, there is a particular trend to take fruit vinegars as part of a healthy lifestyle; popular flavors include lychee, mango, apple, and grape—once diluted with water they are transformed into a refreshing, naturally low-sugar juice.

Whatever the type of fruit vinegar you choose, you will find it sweeter than most other varieties of vinegar, and this makes it a healthier alternative to other vinegars in a vinaigrette dressing as you can cut the calories by using less oil. Fruit vinegars make a delicious choice for summer leaf and vegetable salads, herb sauces, and sprinkled over fresh or poached fruit of any variety. Fruit vinegars are particularly good as marinades for poultry, ham, pork, veal, and fish. You will find they enhance subtle flavors when used in moderation and do not dominate as much as other vinegars.

Oil and Vinegar
Recipes

PAIRING OILS AND VINEGARS

Not all oils and vinegars are destined to be matched with each other, and some are better used on their own. It is easier to mix neutral-tasting oils with the desired vinegar of your choice, but some of the stronger flavored ones can be overpowering, or those with more subtle flavor notes can be lost in an inappropriate match. Here are some of the best and most interesting combinations for dressings and sauces:

OIL	VINEGAR
argan	verjuice
avocado	verjuice, Zinfandel wine, champagne vinegar
brazil nut	raspberry, blueberry, Vincotto®, agridulce
camelina	Chardonnay wine, champagne vinegar
chinese chili	coconut, white or brown rice vinegar, sherry vinegar
hazelnut	champagne vinegar, white balsamic, vinaigre de miel
lemon	verjuice, white balsamic
extra virgin olive	verjuice, balsamic, sherry, Vincotto®, agridulce, bell pepper, carrot, tomato, herb
pecan	balsamic, Vincotto®, agridulce, raspberry, blueberry, fig, sherry, maple
pistachio	verjuice, balsamic, or sherry vinegar
plum seed	verjuice or white balsamic
pumpkin seed	balsamic, Vincotto®, agridulce, fig, Banylus wine, robust red wine
sesame seed	groundnut and rice vinegars, sherry or coconut
walnut	balsamic, Vincotto®, agridulce, raspberry, blueberry, fig, sherry, Banylus, robust red wine, beetroot vinegar

CLASSIC OIL AND VINEGAR RECIPES

As we have seen throughout the directory, oils and vinegars have many applications in the kitchen. Here are a few of the basic methods for making your own infusions and dressings.

Infused Vinegars and Oils

Making your own herb vinegars and oils is quite straightforward. You can use your own favorites, and the basic method is the same whatever you use. However, you must ensure that all the jars and bottles you use are as clean as possible (preferably sterilized) in order to prevent bacterial growth and contamination.

Basic Herb Vinegar

Use cider or white or red wine vinegar as a base depending on your desired use or personal preference. Wash and pat dry the fresh herbs of your choice. Bruise freshly picked leaves by crushing them gently with a rolling pin and loosely press into clean, dry bottles or jars. Pour over sufficient warmed but not hot vinegar to fill the jar. Seal with a non-corrosive, acid-proof lid. Set on a sunny windowsill and shake daily for about 2 weeks. Test for flavor and either store as it is (remembering the flavor will get stronger if you leave the herbs in the vinegar) or strain and rebottle. For a much stronger flavor, strain the herb vinegar and rebottle it with fresh herbs.

Basic Herb Oil

Loosely fill a sterilized bottle with freshly picked herbs as above, and fill with warmed safflower, grapeseed, groundnut, sunflower, red palm oil, or light olive oil. Seal and proceed as for vinegar.

Classic Vinaigrette

In a small bowl or jug, whisk 2 tablespoons wine vinegar, tarragon vinegar, cider, or sherry vinegar with 2 teaspoons Dijon mustard, a pinch of salt, and some ground white or black pepper. Whisk in 6 tablespoons olive oil or more neutral oil if preferred.

Note: Always whisk salt into the vinegar as it will not dissolve in oil. You can replace the vinegar with verjuice (see page 115) to make a more suitable dressing to serve at a meal accompanied by fine wines if preferred.

Honey Mustard Dressing

In a small bowl or jug, whisk 2 tablespoons cider, sherry, or apple vinegar with 2 teaspoons wholegrain mustard, 2 teaspoons clear honey, a pinch of salt, and some ground white or black pepper. Whisk in 6 tablespoons extra virgin rapeseed oil or a neutral oil such as grape nut, safflower, or sunflower.
Variation: Replace 1 teaspoon oil with 1 teaspoon walnut oil.

Oriental Dressing

Put 2 tablespoons sugar in a small screw top jar and add 2 tablespoons white or brown rice vinegar, a crushed garlic clove, and a finely chopped spring onion. Season well, seal, and shake well to mix. Add 1 teaspoon sesame oil or Chinese peanut oil and 6 tablespoons groundnut oil. Shake well again and serve as a dressing for a crisp raw vegetable salad, for steamed fish or chicken, or over freshly cooked rice or noodles.

BERRY VINEGAR

The intense fruitiness of this vinegar works perfectly with olive oil and nut oils.
Makes: approx. 16 fl oz

Cranberry vinegar

INGREDIENTS
1 lb 7 oz fresh raspberries, blackberries, blueberries, cranberries or strawberries, washed and hulled
20 fl oz white wine or cider vinegar

METHOD
1. Place 9 oz of the berries in a non-reactive bowl and pour over the vinegar. Cover and leave for 24 hours in a cool place.
2. The next day, strain the liquid and discard the fruit. Place another 9 oz fruit in a non-reactive bowl and pour over the fruited vinegar. Cover and leave as before.
3. The next day, strain the liquid through cheesecloth and discard the fruit. Put the remaining berries in a large, clean, dry bottle or jar and pour over the fruited vinegar. Seal well and leave to stand in a cool, dark place for at east a month before using.

Variation: Herbs such as bay, rosemary, lemon balm, basil, or tarragon can also be added to the final mix to make a subtle variation of flavor, as can fragrant spices such as cinnamon, cardamom, coriander seeds, or star anise.

LAVENDER VINEGAR

A light floral seasoning to mix with
delicate flavored oils like
sunflower or camelina.
Makes: 16 fl oz

INGREDIENTS

A few sprigs fresh lavender in heavy bud
16 fl oz white balsamic vinegar, champagne,
or good quality white wine vinegar

METHOD

1. Wash and pat dry the lavender sprigs using
   absorbent kitchen paper. Line a board with
   clear wrap and arrange the lavender on top.
   Lay a sheet of baking parchment on top and
   gently crush the lavender using a rolling pin
   to allow the flavor to be extracted. Push into
   clean dry bottles.
2. Lightly warm the vinegar but do not allow
   it to get too hot and pour over the lavender
   to fill the bottle. Seal with a non-corrosive,
   acid-proof lid. Set on a sunny windowsill and
   shake daily for about 2 weeks.
3. Test for flavor and either store as it is
   (remembering the flavor will get stronger)
   or strain and rebottle. For a much stronger
   flavor, strain and rebottle the vinegar with
   more fresh lavender.

Note: This is the same method to use with other
flowering herbs such as lemon balm, lemon- or
rose-scented geranium, and rose petals.

PICKLING VINEGARS

Vinegar is a great medium for preserving
vegetables and fruit. Here are 2
basic recipes for flavored vinegars
suitable for pickling.

SPICED VINEGAR FOR VEGETABLES

Mix 2 tablespoons each of mustard seeds, black
peppercorns, and allspice berries with 1
tablespoon cloves, a small piece of dry root
ginger, grated, and 10 small dried chiles, and
then tie in a small square of clean cheesecloth.
Add to a saucepan containing 20 fl oz malt
vinegar. Bring to a boil and simmer for 10 to 15
minutes depending on how strong you want the
spice flavor to be. Allow to cool, then discard
the spice bag. Bottle and store until required.

SPICED VINEGAR FOR FRUIT

Tie a small cinnamon stick, broken in half, in a
small square of clean cheesecloth with 10
cloves, 1 teaspoon allspice berries, and a piece
of blade mace (optional). Add to a pan
containing 20 fl oz cider or white malt vinegar.
Bring to a boil and simmer for 10 to 15 minutes
depending on how strong you want the spice
flavor to be. Allow to cool then discard the spice
bag. Bottle and store until required.

VINEGAR SAUCE TO SERVE WITH ROAST MEATS

Traditionally this sauce is flavored with fresh mint and served with roast lamb,
but other variations can be made. Fresh thyme makes a good alternative to serve with
guinea fowl, and rosemary is excellent with lamb or game meats. This version
is perfect for roast pork or sausages. Makes: 5 fl oz

INGREDIENTS

3 tbsp freshly chopped sage
1¹/₂ tbsp sugar
2 tbsp boiling water
5 fl oz white wine or cider

METHOD

1. Put the sage in a heatproof non-reactive
   bowl and mix in the sugar. Add the boiling
   water, and stir to dissolve the sugar. Set aside
   to cool.
2. Stir in the vinegar. Mix well, and allow to
   stand at room temperature for 30 minutes
   before serving.

GARLIC OIL

A rich flavored oil that combines with more robust vinegars like beer or red wine or even balsamic. Makes: 20 fl oz

INGREDIENTS

2 sprigs fresh thyme
2 sprigs fresh rosemary
2 bay leaves
4 cloves garlic, unpeeled
20 fl oz light olive, grapeseed, red palm oil, safflower, or sunflower oil

METHOD

1. Wash and pat dry the herbs using absorbent kitchen paper. Push into clean, dry bottles.
2. Lightly warm the oil but do not allow it to get too hot and pour over the herbs and garlic to fill the bottle. Seal with a non-corrosive lid. Set on a sunny windowsill and shake daily for about 2 weeks.
3. Test for flavor and either store as it is (remembering the flavor will get stronger) or strain and rebottle. For a much stronger flavor, strain and rebottle with more fresh herbs and garlic.

Note: While oil can be flavored by adding other aromatics such as broiled bell peppers, onions, and chiles to it for an extended period of time, extra care must be taken when using, and subsequently storing, such oils in order to prevent the growth of *Clostridium botulinum* (the bacteria that produces toxins that can lead to botulism) in this medium. Store well sealed in a cool, dark place—if in doubt, keep refrigerated—and use within 3 months.

MAYONNAISE

If you want to flavor your mayonnaise with olive oil, choose an extra virgin oil and use $^1/_3$ to $^1/_2$ olive oil to safflower or sunflower. Makes: approx. 7 fl oz

INGREDIENTS

1 medium organic egg yolk
$^1/_2$ tsp dry mustard powder
$^1/_2$ tsp salt
pinch of ground white pepper
$^1/_2$ tsp sugar
approx. 5 fl oz light olive oil, safflower, sunflower oil, grapeseed, red palm oil, or groundnut oil
1 tbsp tarragon wine vinegar, white wine, cider, or sherry vinegar

METHOD

1. Place the egg yolk in a bowl with the mustard, salt, pepper, and sugar. Mix well.
2. Add the oil, drop by drop, whisking until thick, smooth, and glossy. If the mixture "splits" or curdles, put another egg yolk in a basin and gradually add the split mixture as above.
3. When sufficient oil has been added, carefully fold in the vinegar and mix thoroughly. Cover and chill until required. Keep refrigerated and use within 5 days.

VARIATION

For a touch of nuttiness use groundnut oil as your base oil and replace 2 tablespoons with the same amount of walnut, hazelnut, avocado, pecan, or macadamia nut oil. For a sesame, hemp, or pumpkin seed flavor, replace 2 teaspoons groundnut oil with the seed oil of your choice. For a golden, slightly nutty mayonnaise, use extra virgin rapeseed oil.

WALNUT AND GOAT'S CHEESE PESTO

This pesto is delicious stirred into freshly cooked pasta or rice, or spread over fish or chicken before baking. Makes: approx. 7 oz

INGREDIENTS
1 garlic clove, peeled and crushed
½ oz fresh parsley sprigs, washed and dried
4 oz shelled walnuts
2 oz mild goat's cheese, crumbled
4 tbsp walnut oil
salt and freshly ground black pepper

METHOD
1. Place all the ingredients in a blender or food processor and blend for a few seconds until they are smooth.
2. Season to taste and transfer to a sealed container and store in the fridge for up to 7 days.

VARIATION
For a classic Italian pesto sauce, replace the parsley with basil, the goat's cheese with Parmesan, the walnuts for pine nuts, and use extra virgin olive oil instead. Season to taste.

SUPPLIERS

www.ambrosia-foods.com
www.bmausa.net
www.boyajianinc.com
www.chefshop.com
www.cookingbuddies.com
www.delectable.com
www.dellalpe.com
www.elikioliveoil.com
www.gourmeton.com
www.honestfoods.com
www.igourmet.com
www.jrmushroomsandspecialties.com
www.kushistore.com
www.latourangelle.com
www.lepicerie.com
www.maggiebeer.com.au
www.mannpacking.com

www.nowfoods.com
www.olivado.com
www.penmac.com
www.piermallstore.com
www.plumgoodfood.com
www.primoolio.com
www.raos.com
www.rawoils.com
www.republicoftea.com
www.sanfranciscobrewcraft.com
www.savorypantry.com
www.simply-natural.biz
www.spigroup.net
www.taylorsmarket.com
www.viansa.com
www.wabashvalleyfarms.com
www.zestgourmet.com

BIBLIOGRAPHY

Briggs, Margaret, *Vinegar—1001 Practical Uses*, Abbeydale Press, 2007
Davidson, Alan, *The Oxford Companion of Food*, OUP, 1999
Faber, Lee, *Healthy Oils*, Abbeydale Press, 2007
Kipple and Ornelas, *The Cambridge World History of Food Volume One and Volume Two*, CUP, 2000
Larousse Gastronomique, Paul Hamlyn, 1989

McGee, Harold, *McGee On Food and Cooking*, Hodder & Stoughton, 2004
Smith, Andrew F., *The Oxford Encyclopaedia of Food and Drink in America*, OUP, 2004
Stobart, Tom, *The Cook's Encyclopaedia*, Papermac, 1982

ACKNOWLEDGMENTS

Special thanks to Stephen and Greta Brown of McNees, Crieff and to Diane Brown of Provender Brown, Perth, for their help in supplying specific products for my research.

INDEX

INDEX

INDEX / PICTURE CREDITS

PICTURE CREDITS

PICTURE CREDITS

Shutterstock
46. Canola oil, rapeseed pods and seeds, © Kröger/ Gross / StockFood UK
47. Oil popped popcorn, © OlgaLis / Shutterstock
48. Poppy seed oil, © Klauss Arras / StockFood UK; poppy seeds, © Kröger/Gross / StockFood UK
49. Tea oil, © Carolgaranda / Shutterstock; Tea fruit, © TH Foto / StockFood UK
50. Pumpkin seed oil with pumpkin slice and seeds, © FoodPhotogr. Eising / StockFood UK
51. Hemp seed oil and hemp seeds, © Quintet Publishing
53. Silk cotton tree, © Photomediacom / Shutterstock
54. Avocado oil and avocadoes, © Quintet Publishing
55. Avocado and cherry tomato salad drizzled with avocado oil, © Foodcollection / StockFood UK
56. Cotton seed oil, © National Cotton Seed Products Association, Inc.
58. Selección especial Carbonell, © Quintet Publishing
59. L'Olio lizzanello ginni Calogiuri, © Quintet Publishing; Carapelli Firenze, © Quintet Publishing
60. Filippo Berio Mild and Light Oil, © Quintet Publishing; Filippo Berio Gusto Fruttato, © Quintet Publishing
61. Filippo Berio Gusto Fruttato, © Quintet Publishing
62. Dauro de L'Epoda, © Quintet Publishing; Valderrama Estate, © Quintet Publishing; Ionis Kalamatra, © Quintet Publishing
63. So! Gourmet, © Quintet Publishing; Cobram Estate, © Quintet Publishing
64. Extra virgin olive oil with balsamic vinegar and fresh Italian bread, © Eugene Bochkarev / Shutterstock
65. Olives on the tree, © Condor36 / Shutterstock
66. Coconut oil and coconut, © Quintet Publishing
67. Coconut palm tree, © Hannamariah / Shutterstock; Coconuts, © Jovan Nikolic / Shutterstock
68. Rice bran oil and rice grains, © Quintet Publishing
69. Close-up of rice plant, © Frank Di Luzio / StockFood UK
70. Pili nuts, © inga spence / Alamy
73. Perilla plant and flowers, © Steven Forster Group, Ic. / StockFood UK
74. Sunflower Oil with sunflower seeds, © Quintet Publishing
75. A field of sunflowers, © mypokcik / Shutterstock
78. Mustard flower in bloom, © Joellen L Armstrong / Shutterstock
79. Mustard seed oil and mustard seeds, © Quintet Publishing
80. Safflower oil with safflower seeds, © Quintet Publishing
81. Plum seed oil and plums, © Quintet Publishing
83. Açai berries with leaves, © Paul Williams / StockFood UK
84. Wheat germ oil with wheat germ, © Quintet Publishing
85. Vegetable oil, © Quintet Publishing; Sunflower, © JUPITERIMAGES / Brand X / Alamy
87. Babassu palm nuts, © Luiz Claudio / Nature Picture Library
88. Soybean oil with soybeans, © Quintet Publishing

89. Edamame, © Lew Robertson / StockFood UK
90. Palm oil and palm oil kernel, © Quintet Publishing
91. Carotino red palm and canola oil, © Quintet Publishing
93. Corn oil, © Quintet Publishing; Sweetcorn, © Shutterstock
94. Conimex Wok Oil, © Quintet Publishing; Rustichella D'Abruzzo Linon Olio, © Quintet Publishing
95. Cool chile co Cipotle Chile oil, © Quintet Publishing; Gocce Di Peccato al Tartufo Nero, © Quintet Publishing
96. Storing vinegar in barrels, © Shutterstock
97. Vinegar used for pickling, © Shutterstock
98. Balsamic vinegar and olive oil, © Shutterstock
99. Advertisement for Champion's Vinegar, © Mary Evans Picture Library / Alamy
101. Vinegar production, © Alamy
102. Vinegar decanted into glasses, © Shutterstock
103. Vinegar and cloves of garlic, © Vasyl Helevachuk / Shutterstock
104. Vinagre de Reims Clovis, © Quintet Publishing; Vino vinaigre de Chardonnay, © Quintet Publishing
105. Wine vinegar, © Cephas Picture Library / Alamy
106. Chianti wine vinegar, © Quintet Publishing; Vino Moscatel wine vinegar, © Quintet Publishing
107. Unio Vermouth wine vinegar, © Quintet Publishing; Martin Pouret aged red wine vinegar, © Quintet Publishing
108. Gran deposito aceto balsamico di moderna gioseppe giusti, © Quintet Publishing
109. Acetaia sereni Balsamic vinegar de Modena, © Quintet Publishing
110. French bread, oil and balsamic vinegar, © Pinkcandy / Shutterstock
111. Bouquet methode balsamique fig bouquet, © Quintet Publishing
112. White balsamic vinegar, © Quintet Publishing
113. Vincotto®, © Quintet Publishing
114. Agridulce di Chardonnay vinegar, © Quintet Publishing; Agridulce de Cabernet Sauvignon vinegar, © Quintet Publishing
115. Verjuice, © drKaczmar / Shutterstock
116. Martin Pouret red wine vinegar, © Quintet Publishing
117. The capital of vinegar, Orleans on the Loire river in France, © Alamy
118. Clovis Sherry Vinegar Reserva, © Quintet Publishing
119. Vintage Superior Sherry wine vinegar, © Quintet Publishing
120. Waitrose cider vinegar, © Quintet Publishing; Vinaigre de cidre de Normandie, © Quintet Publishing
121. Perry vinegar, © Quintet Publishing; Kuhne exquisite apple vinegar, © Quintet Publishing
122. Raisin vinegar, © Quintet Publishing; Date vinegar, © Nikola Bilic / Shutterstock; Dates, Karl Newedel / StockFood UK
123. Dates on tree, © Vera Bogaerts / Shutterstock
124. UFC CoCo vinegar, © Quintet Publishing
125. UFC Native vinegar, © Quintet Publishing
127. Palm tree, © Tatiana Morozova / Shutterstock
128. Sarsons Distiled malt vinegar, © Quintet Publishing; Sarsons malt vinegar, © Quintet

Publishing
129. Casa Perdido malt vinegar, © Quintet Publishing; White vinegar, © Quintet Publishing; fish and chips, © Jenny Horne / Shutterstock
130. Rice fields, © Lim Yong Hian / Shutterstock
131. Marukan genuine brewed rice vinegar, © Quintet Publishing
132. Chinese black vinegar, © Quintet Publishing
133. Chinese red vinegar, © Quintet Publishing; Chinese white vinegar, © Quintet Publishing
134. Japanese brown rice vinegar, © Quintet Publishing
135. Yutaka Japanese rice vinegar, © Quintet Publishing
136. Datu Puti cane vinegar, © Quintet Publishing; Sukang Maasim, © Quintet Publishing
137. Honey vinegar and honeycomb, © Shutterstock
138. Whey and whey powder, © Karl Newedel / StockFood UK
139. Yuzu fruit on the Yuzu tree, Japan, Yamanashi Prefecture, Masuho, Mt Fuji, © Getty Images
140. Suka vinegar, © Quintet Publishing
141. Kombucha vinegar, © L'Immaginario / StockFood UK
142. Maple vinegar, © Klaus Arras / StockFood UK; maple leaves, © Ottmar Diez / StockFood UK
143. Maille wine vinegar with Tarragon, © Quintet Publishing; Vinaigre Saveur Menthe Verte, © Quintet Publishing
144. Fischerauer Karotten Essig, © Quintet Publishing
145. Lemon vinegar, © Quintet Publishing
146. Clearspring Japanese ume plum seasoning, © Quintet Publishing
147. Oil and vinegar recipes, © Alamy
149. Salad dressing, © Alamy
150. Cranberry vinegar, © Jip Fens / Shutterstock; raspberries, © SasPartout / Shutterstock
151. Lavender, © joanna wnuk / Shutterstock; Pickling vinegars, © Alamy
152. Vinegar sauce, © Shutterstock; Fresh mint leaves, © Brian Chase / Shutterstock
153. Garlic oil, © Alamy; Garlic cloves, © SteveSPF / Shutterstock
154. Mayonnaise, © Pawel Strykowski / Shutterstock; Mayonnaise, © Alamy
155. Walnut and goat's cheese salad, © H. D. Connelly / Shutterstock; walnuts, © PhotoCreate / Shutterstock